Madeline Cavenagh

A Florida Sand Dollar Book

PALMETTO LEAVES

HARRIET BEECHER STOWE

with Introductions by Mary B. Graff
and Edith Cowles

University Press of Florida

GAINESVILLE TALLAHASSEE TAMPA BOCA RATON
PENSACOLA ORLANDO MIAMI JACKSONVILLE

Facsimile reproduction of the 1873 edition
New material (introductions and index) copyright 1968
by the Board of Regents of the State of Florida
First paperback printing, 1999
Printed in the United States of America on acid-free paper

07 06 05 04 03   6 5 4 3 2

Library of Congress Cataloging-in-Publication Data
Stowe, Harriet Beecher, 1811–1896.
Palmetto leaves / Harriet Beecher Stowe: with introductions
by Mary B. Graff and Edith Cowles.
p.cm.
Reprint. Originally published: Boston: J. F. Osgood and Co., 1873.
With new introd.
ISBN 0-8130-1693-2 (pbk.: alk. paper)
1. Saint Johns River Valley (Fla.)—Description and travel. 2. Mandarin
(Fla.)—Social life and customs—19th century. 3. Saint Johns River
Valley (Fla.)—Social life and customs—19th century. 4. Mandarin
(Fla.)—Social life and customs—19th century. 5. Stowe, Harriet
Beecher, 1811–1896. I. Title.
F317.S2S8 1999
975.9'061—dc21 98-53476

The University Press of Florida is the scholarly publishing
agency for the State University System of Florida, comprising
Florida A & M University, Florida Atlantic University, Florida
International University, Florida State University, University of
Central Florida, University of Florida, University of North Florida,
University of South Florida, and University of West Florida.

University Press of Florida
15 Northwest 15th Street
Gainesville, FL 32611
http://www.upf.com

THE AUTHOR

THE seventh child of strict Calvinist parents, Harriet Elizabeth Beecher Stowe was born June 14, 1811, in Litchfield, Connecticut. Her father, Lyman Beecher, was the pastor of the local Congregational church. Roxana Foote, the minister's first wife and the mother of five sons and three daughters, died when Harriet was only four. Roxana's influence continued throughout the lives of the children. Because of her pious character she wished that all of her sons might enter the ministry, and with one exception, Harriet's five brothers did become ministers.

Harriet herself could hardly escape a concern

for theology. When she was thirteen years old she wrote a composition entitled "Can the Immortality of the Soul be Proved by the Light of the Nature?" in which she defended this thesis. As the school's guest of honor, her father praised the essay although he did not know that his own daughter had written it. "It was the proudest moment of my life," Harriet recalled.

In the fall of 1824 Harriet left her birthplace to attend the Hartford (Connecticut) Female Seminary, a school established by her stern twenty-three-year-old sister Catherine. Here Harriet was both pupil and teacher.

Lyman Beecher was elected president of the newly founded Lane Theological Seminary in 1830, and the family moved to Cincinnati in 1832. Harriet's letters to friends back home revealed her excitement in the new environment which her father called "the London of the West." Employed now as a teacher in her sister's latest establishment, the Western Female Institute, Harriet found time to write a few magazine sketches, sentimental stories, and to receive a prize of fifty dollars for "A New England Sketch." The story appeared in the April, 1834, issue of the *Western Monthly Magazine*.

In 1836 when she married the young widower Calvin Ellis Stowe, a Greek and Hebrew scholar, her serious efforts toward a writing career were somewhat curtailed. Juggling her duties as wife and mother, she did manage to keep her hand in; but the few sketches published in 1843 aroused little public notice. Their potential, however, convinced her husband that she must aim for recognition, and he urged her to establish herself as Harriet Beecher Stowe, "a name euphonious, flowing, and full of meaning."

During the Stowes' eighteen years in Cincinnati, where six of their seven children were born and one was buried, Harriet was an exhausted housewife, harassed by debt, personal sorrows, and family difficulties.

Better days came in 1850, when Calvin Stowe accepted a professorship at his alma mater, Bowdoin College, and moved his family to Brunswick, Maine. Despite the passage of the Fugitive Slave Law and the prodding of friends and relatives who urged Harriet to enter the public debate, she continued to write only the mild sketches with which she had long been identified. Only one article, "The Freedman's Dream: A Parable," mentioned the slavery issue. She wrote what was pleasing and profitable, for throughout most of her married life she was to supplement her husband's meager income. It was a compromise and she knew it: "If I choose to be a literary lady, I have, I think, as good a chance of making profit by it as any one I know of."

A nudge from her editor extended her scope. In complying with the suggestion of Gamaliel

Bailey, editor of the *National Era*, Harriet enlarged a short story about the death of an old slave. *Uncle Tom's Cabin: or Life Among the Lowly*, which was to weave her destiny into the fabric of a national issue, thus began as a serial on June 5, 1851. And what was to be four installments ran to fifty.

Its impact zoomed. The book was published in 1852, and three thousand copies were sold the first day; within a year more than three hundred thousand copies were sold. Despite the immediate success of *Uncle Tom's Cabin*, Mrs. Stowe was financially no better off. The book did assure her a bargaining position in publishing circles: she no longer needed to ask editors to consider her manuscripts, nor did she have to beg for advances on unwritten stories.

Now, however, she had to cope with further demands: maintaining a reputation and facing public criticism. The excitement of success was one thing; the weariness of unresolved household problems was another. She began to look for differences.

Early in 1866 she was seriously considering a winter residence in Florida. To her brother Charles Beecher she wrote: "My plan of going to Florida, as it lies in my mind, is not in any sense a worldly enterprise. . . . My heart is with that poor people whose course in words I have tried to plead, and who now, ignorant and docile, are just in that formative stage in which whoever seizes has them."

Mrs. Stowe's attention had been turned toward Florida for some time. In 1866 she had established her son Frederick on "Laurel Grove," an old plantation located on the west side of the St. Johns River, near the town of Orange Park. Having advanced $10,000 to rent a thousand-acre cotton experiment which was to provide work opportunities for freed Negroes, she decided to check on her investment and to show a mother's concern for a wayward son.

What she discovered at Laurel Grove disappointed her, but the three weeks she spent at Orange Park in March and April of 1867 convinced her that Florida offered real advantages as a winter residence.

One day she and Frederick rowed to a settlement on the opposite side of the river, where they picked up their mail. This excursion gave Mrs. Stowe her first sight of Mandarin. Since she liked what she encountered, she began to investigate available property.

She first approached her brother Charles Beecher: "I am now in correspondence with the Bishop of Florida, with a view to establishing a line of churches along the St. John's River, and if I settle at Mandarin, it will be one of my stations. Will you consent to enter the Episcopal Church and be our clergyman? You are just the man we want. . . ." Although Charles did not comply with his sister's proposal, he did come to Florida to settle on the St. Marks River at Newport, about twenty miles from Tallahassee.

In 1867 Mrs. Stowe purchased thirty acres of the "Old Fairbanks Grant." There was a modest cottage on a bluff overlooking the St. Johns River for her winter home in Mandarin. The Stowes' house, with its porch built around one of the moss-hung live oak trees, became the most photographed residence in the community. An orange grove behind the house delighted Mrs. Stowe, whose pleasure increased when local growers assured her that the crop would yield $2,000 annually.

Throughout the spring of 1868 signs of a love affair between the land and the enterprising lady glowed in her letters. Mrs. Stowe was so taken by the semitropical aspects and what she called the "calm isle of Patmos" that she could ignore her impatient publisher. She was finding new outlets for her energies.

Her enthusiasm was catching. By 1869 she had persuaded her cousin Spencer Foote and his family to move to Mandarin and manage her grove. The partnership succeeded. Orange crates headed for northern markets carried proof that the Stowes' name was getting top billing in the bold stenciled letters: "Oranges from HARRIET BEECHER STOWE, MANDARIN, FLA."

There were other activities. Playing hookey from routine writing, she relished the variety and charm of village square dances, picnics, and theatrical productions. It was not in her nature, however, to detach herself from causes in which she strongly believed. Early in their idyllic Mandarin episode, the Stowes had devoted much of their time to the religious education of children, both white and colored. That the family was uniquely versed for this endeavor pleased Mrs.

Stowe. She had written Annie Fields, "We had minister, organist, and choir all in our own family, we were sure of them at all events."

Deeply concerned with the church activities, she worked hard to secure financial support for the program. But to rely on friends—whom she often badgered for contributions—was neither an easy nor an effective way to maintain a personal charity in an unknown village.

Besides, her own financial needs were again pressing. She had invested thirty-four thousand dollars in various ways, none of which would give her immediate income. Furthermore, she could no longer hope for her husband to add to their income, since she had urged him to retire. She confided her anxieties to John R. Howard, who was a member of the John Bruce Ford publishing firm and one of the editors of the newly organized *Christian Union*.

What evolved from her arrangement with

Howard was to alleviate somewhat the stress of inadequate income. Any pieces she wrote were almost certain to find a place in the *Christian Union*.

With this reassuring agreement she devoted her leisure—and she had more of it now that her twin daughters assumed responsibility for the household chores—to a variety of topics, many of which declared her enthusiasm for Florida. By the winter of 1872 she had so directed her energies toward the pursuit of this happiness that she offered to James R. Osgood, not the novel he had requested, but a series of sketches entitled *Palmetto Leaves*.

This was probably the first unsolicited promotion writing to interest the northern tourist in Florida. In the slender volume Mrs. Stowe, besides giving an intimate glimpse of her own life in Mandarin, painted a picture of Florida as a tropical paradise. For her the charm of this winter-summer land was "to be able to spend your winter out of doors, even though some days be cold; to be able to sit with windows open; to hear birds daily; to eat fruit from trees, and pick flowers from hedges, all winter long." That she took credit for arousing interest in her claims for Florida was apparent in her report to Annie Fields that fourteen thousand tourists had visited the state that [1873] year.

For the Stowes the years spent in Florida were full of contentment. They were entranced by the charm and congeniality of life in Mandarin and were sincere in their desire to become a part of a new life. They gave their strength and efforts to the building of this old-new village, for here they lived simply and fully among friends who respected and accepted them as individuals and not as celebrities.

Six years before Calvin Stowe's death in 1886, Mrs. Stowe began the task of sorting, discarding, and arranging the great accumulation of letters and papers relating to her life. She gave her selections to her son, Charles Edward Stowe, to write the official biography. Her long and productive life ended, at the age of eighty-five, on July 1, 1896.

MARY B. GRAFF

THE TEXT

WE know that fact and fantasy have often intermingled in the voices of Florida's advocates. To be teased by the prospects of a rejuvenated pulse or an inflated purse has such universal appeal that the purveyors of Bali Hai and El Dorado have often made hay in the Land of Sunshine.

Harriet Beecher Stowe was one of Florida's early promoters. Effusive as she sometimes was in her response to the wild charms of the land, she allowed no ballyhoo to nuzzle her claims for Nature's legacy. What she proposed she practiced: open covenant with the open skies. With the propriety of an earnest midwife she urged the cutting of ties and the efficacy of change.

Although *Palmetto Leaves* is a narrow portrait of a landscape on and around the St. Johns River, it gives vigorous proof of Mrs. Stowe's ability to wheedle advantage out of differences. She liked the activity that helped her pay her bills, and it is apparent that these passages to solvency were rallying salvos of a joyous and pragmatic nature. Were we whipped by the rigors of northern winters and the debilities of age some ninety years ago, her call "to come down here once, and use your own eyes, and you will know more than we can teach you" would not end as a specious injunction to exchange familiar woes for a warranted paradise. She was aware that invalids seeking miracles often came to southern climes too late. And she had a ready answer for a doctor who blamed the swamps: "As to malaria, it is not necessary to souse Manhattan Island under water to get *that* in and around New York."

"It is not to be denied," she wrote, "that full

half of the tourists and travelers that come to Florida return intensely disappointed, and even disgusted. Why?—Evidently because Florida, like a piece of embroidery, has two sides to it— one side all tag-rag and thrums, without order or position; and the other side showing flowers and arabesques and brilliant coloring. Both these sides exist. Both are undeniable, undisputed facts, not only in the case of Florida, but of every place and thing under the sun."

Like a well-tempered disputant, Mrs. Stowe reminded those romantic tourists that "In New England, Nature is an up and down, smart, decisive house-mother, that has her times and seasons and brings up her ends of life with a positive jerk. She will have no shilly-shally. When her time comes, she cleans off the gardens and forests thoroughly and once for all, and they are clean. Then she freezes the ground solid as iron; and then she covers all up with a nice pure winding-sheet of snow; and seals matters up as a good housewife does her jelly tumblers under white paper covers. . . . Nature down here," she continued, "is an easy, demoralized, indulgent old grandmother who has no particular time for anything, and does everything when she happens to feel like it."

Admonishing her northern friends "to accept certain deficiencies as the necessary shadow to certain excellences," she confessed that the Stowes were "getting reconciled to a sort of tumble-down, wild, picnicky kind of life. . . . If we painted her [Florida] she would be a brunette, dark but comely, with gorgeous tissues, a general disarray and dazzle, and with a sort of jolly untidiness, free, easy, and joyous."

Many of the pieces in *Palmetto Leaves* were responses to inquiries which Mrs. Stowe preferred to answer "in the gross, and through *The Christian Union,*" where many of them originally appeared. For the most part her correspondents requested information about the climate, the cost of lodgings ("The prices of board at Green Cove Springs, Magnolia, and Hibernia vary all the way from twelve to thirty-five dollars per week"), the cultivation of oranges, and the availability of land. One inquirer, eager to know about government land in Florida, learned that "thousands of acres of good land, near to a market, near to a great river on which 3 or 4 steamboats are daily plying, can be had for five dollars per acre, and for even less than that."

Although Mrs. Stowe was sufficiently informed to supply useful data, she exercised an appealing independence in choosing her topics: "One must write what one is thinking of. When the mind is full of one thing, why go about to write on another?"

One is inclined to agree, for Mrs. Stowe, keenly responsive to those "gorgeous tissues," kept her mind filled with a number of things: adventures in the woods with flowers and trees and birds; observations about life among Negroes finding their way out of slavery; projected enterprises in farms and dairies; and a deep affection for the St. Johns River, "the great blue sheet of water [that] shimmers and glitters like so much liquid lapis lazuli."

Occasionally she tossed the exclamation point where nothing stirred, but more often when her subject controlled her style (such as her analysis of plant and animal growths on page 73), she wrote with accuracy and force.

Throughout these pieces, whatever the topic, the refreshing awareness of this Connecticut Yankee in a land she marveled at may prompt many a modern reader to question the shrunken dimensions of his own zest for living.

EDITH COWLES

PALMETTO-LEAVES

BY

HARRIET BEECHER STOWE.

ILLUSTRATED.

BOSTON :

JAMES R. OSGOOD AND COMPANY,

(LATE TICKNOR & FIELDS, AND FIELDS, OSGOOD, & CO.)

1873.

Boston:
Stereotyped and Printed by Rand, Avery, & Co.

CONTENTS.

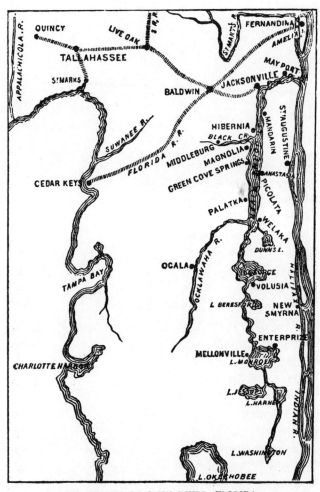

MAP OF THE ST. JOHN RIVER, FLORIDA.

NOBODY'S DOG.

YES, here he comes again! Look at him! Whose dog is he? We are sitting around the little deck-house of the Savannah steamer, in that languid state of endurance which befalls voyagers, when, though the sky is clear, and the heavens blue, and the sea calm as a looking-glass, there is yet that gentle, treacherous, sliding rise and fall, denominated a ground-swell.

Reader, do you remember it? Of all deceitful demons of the deep, this same smooth, slippery, cheating ground-swell is the most diabolic. Because, you see, he is a *mean* imp, an underhanded, unfair, swindling scamp, who takes from you all the glory of endurance. Fair to the eye, plausible as possible, he says to you, "What's the matter? What can you ask brighter than this sky, smoother than this sea, more glossy and calm than these rippling waves? How fortunate that you have such an exceptionally smooth voyage!"

And yet look around the circle of pale faces fixed in that grim expression of endurance, the hands belonging to them resolutely clasping lemons, — those looks of unutterable, repressed disgust and endurance. Are these people seasick? Oh, no! of course not. "Of course," says the slippery, plausible demon, "these people can't be sick in this delightful weather, and with this delightful, smooth sea!"

But here comes the dog, now slowly drooping from one to another, — the most woe-begone
and dejected of all possible dogs. Not a bad-
looking dog, either; not without signs about him
of good dog blood.

We say one to another, as we languidly review
his points, "His hair is fine and curly : he has
what might be a fine tail, were it not drooping in
such abject dejection and discouragement. Evidently this is a dog that has seen better days, —
a dog that has belonged to somebody, and taken
kindly to petting." His long nose, and great
limpid, half-human eyes, have a suggestion of
shepherd-dog blood about them.

He comes and seats himself opposite, and
gazes at you with a pitiful, wistful, intense gaze,
as much as to say, "Oh ! *do* you know where
HE is ? and how came I here ? — poor, miserable
dog that I am !" He walks in a feeble, discouraged way to the wheel-house, and sniffs at the

salt water that spatters there; gives one lick, and stops, and comes and sits quietly down again: it's "no go."

"Poor fellow! he's thirsty," says one; and the Professor, albeit not the most nimble of men, climbs carefully down the cabin-stairs for a tumbler of water, brings it up, and places it before him. Eagerly he laps it all up; and then, with the confiding glance of a dog not unused to kindness, looks as if he would like more. Another of the party fills his tumbler, and he drinks that.

"Why, poor fellow, see how thirsty he was!" "I wonder whose dog he is?" "Somebody ought to see to this dog!" are comments passing round among the ladies, who begin throwing him bits of biscuit, which he snaps up eagerly.

"He's hungry too. Only see how hungry he is! Nobody feeds this dog. Whom does he belong to?"

One of the ship's stewards, passing, throws in a remark, " That dog's seasick : that's what's the matter with him. It won't do to feed that dog ; it won't : it'll make terrible work."

Evidently some stray dog, that has come aboard the steamer by accident, — looking for a lost master, perhaps ; and now here he is alone and forlorn. Nobody's dog !

One of the company, a gentle, fair-haired young girl, begins stroking his rough, dusty hair, which though fine, and capable of a gloss if well kept, now is full of sticks and straws. An unseemly patch of tar disfigures his coat on one side, which seems to worry him : for he bites at it now and then aimlessly ; then looks up with a hopeless, appealing glance, as much as to say, " I know I am looking like a fright ; but I can't help it. Where is HE ? and where am I ? and what does it all mean ? "

But the caresses of the fair-haired lady inspire

him with a new idea. He will be "nobody's dog" no longer: he will choose a mistress.

From that moment he is like a shadow to the fair-haired lady: he follows her steps everywhere, mournful, patient, with drooping tail and bowed head, as a dog not sure of his position, but humbly determined to have a mistress if dogged faith and persistency can compass it. She walks the deck; and tick, tick, pitapat, go the four little paws after her. She stops: he stops, and looks wistful. Whenever and wherever she sits down, he goes and sits at her feet, and looks up at her with eyes of unutterable entreaty.

The stewards passing through the deck-house give him now and then a professional kick; and he sneaks out of one door only to walk quietly round a corner and in at the other, and place himself at her feet. Her party laugh, and rally her on her attractions. She now and then pats

and caresses and pities him, and gives him
morsels of biscuit out of her stores. Evidently
she belongs to the band of dog-lovers. In the
tedious dulness of the three-days' voyage the dog
becomes a topic, and his devotion to the fair-
haired lady an engrossment.

We call for his name. The stewards call him
" Jack :" but he seems to run about as well for
one name as another ; and it is proposed to call
him " Barnes," from the name of the boat we
are on. The suggestion drops, from want of
energy in our very demoralized company to
carry it. Not that we are seasick, one of us :
oh, no ! Grimly upright, always at table, and
eating our three meals a day, who dares intimate
that we are sick ? Perish the thought ! It is
only a dizzy, headachy dulness, with an utter
disgust for every thing in general, that creeps
over us ; and Jack's mournful face reflects but
too truly our own internal troubles.

But at last here we are at Savannah and the Scriven House ; and the obliging waiters rush out and take us in and do for us with the most exhaustive attention. Here let us remark on the differences in hotels. In some you are waited on sourly, in some grudgingly, in some carelessly, in some with insolent negligence. At the Scriven House you are received like long-expected friends. Every thing is at your hand, and the head waiter arranges all as benignantly as if he were really delighted to make you comfortable. So we had a golden time at the Scriven House, where there is every thing to make the wayfarer enjoy himself.

Poor Jack was overlooked in the bustle of the steamer and the last agonies of getting landed. We supposed we had lost sight of him forever. But lo! when the fair-haired lady was crossing the hall to her room, a dog, desperate and dusty, fought his way through the ranks of waiters to get to her.

" It isn't our dog ; put him out gently ; don't hurt him," said the young lady's father.

But Jack was desperate, and fought for his mistress, and bit the waiter that ejected him, and of course got kicked with emphasis into the street.

The next morning, one of our party, looking out of the window, saw Jack watching slyly outside of the hotel. Evidently he was waiting for an opportunity to cast himself at the feet of his chosen protectress.

" If I can only see her, all will yet be right," he says to himself.

We left Savannah in the cars that afternoon ; and the last we heard of Jack, he had been seen following the carriage of his elected mistress in a drive to Bonaventure.

What was the end of the poor dog's romance we have never heard. Whether he is now blessed in being somebody's dog, — petted, cared for,

caressed, — or whether he roves the world deso-
late-hearted as " nobody's dog," with no rights
to life, liberty, or pursuit of happiness, we have
no means of knowing.

But the measureless depth of dumb sorrow,
want, woe, entreaty, that there are in a wandering dog's eyes, is something that always speaks
much to us, — dogs in particular which seem to
leave their own kind to join themselves to man,
and only feel their own being complete when
they have formed a human friendship. It seems
like the ancient legends of those incomplete
natures, a little below humanity, that needed a
human intimacy to develop them. How much
dogs suffer mentally is a thing they have no
words to say; but there is no sorrow deeper than
that in the eyes of a homeless, friendless, mas-
terless dog. We rejoice, therefore, to learn that
one portion of the twenty thousand dollars
which the ladies of Boston have raised for " Our

Dumb Animals " is about to be used in keeping a *home* for stray dogs.

Let no one sneer at this. If, among the " five sparrows sold for two farthings," not one is forgotten by our Father, certainly it becomes us not to forget the poor dumb companions of our mortal journey, capable, with us, of love and its sorrows, of faithfulnesss and devotion. There is, we are told, a dog who haunts the station at Revere, daily looking for the return of a master he last saw there, and who, alas ! will never return. There are, many times and oft, dogs strayed from families, accustomed to kindness and petting, who have lost all they love, and have none to care for them. To give such a refuge, till they find old masters or new, seems only a part of Christian civilization.

The more Christ's spirit prevails, the more we feel for all that can feel and suffer. The poor brute struggles and suffers with us, companion

of our mysterious travel in this lower world; and
who has told us that he may not make a step
upward in the beyond? For our own part, we
like that part of the poor Indian's faith, —

> "That thinks, admitted to yon equal sky,
>   His faithful dog shall bear him company."

So much for poor Jack. Now for Savannah.
It is the prettiest of Southern cities, laid out in
squares, planted with fine trees, and with a series
of little parks intersecting each street, so that
one can walk on fine walks under trees quite
through the city, down to a larger park at the
end of all. Here there is a fountain whose
charming sculpture reminds one of those in the
south of France. A belt of ever-blooming
violets encircles it; and a well-kept garden of
flowers, shut in by an evergreen hedge, surrounds
the whole. It is like a little bit of Paris, and
strikes one refreshingly who has left New York
two days before in a whirling snow-storm.

The thing that every stranger in Savannah goes to see, as a matter of course, is Bonaventure.

This is an ancient and picturesque estate, some miles from the city, which has for years been used as a cemetery.

How shall we give a person who has never seen live-oaks or gray moss an idea of it?

Solemn avenues of these gigantic trees, with their narrow evergreen leaves, their gnarled, contorted branches feathered with ferns and parasitic plants, and draped with long swaying draperies of this gray, fairy-like moss, impress one singularly. The effect is solemn and unearthly; and the distant tombs, urns, and obelisks gleaming here and there among the shadows make it more impressive.

Beneath the trees, large clumps of palmetto, with their waving green fans, give a tropical suggestion to the scene; while yellow jessamine

wreathe and clamber from tree to tree, or weave
mats of yellow blossoms along the ground. It
seems a labyrinth of fairy grottoes, and is in
its whole impression something so unique, that
no one should on any account miss of seeing it.

Savannah is so pleasant a city, and the hotels
there are so well kept, that many find it far
enough south for all their purposes, and spend
the winter there. But we are bound farther
towards the equator, and so here we ponder the
question of our onward journey.

A railroad with Pullman sleeping-cars takes
one in one night from Savannah to Jacksonville,
Fla.; then there is a steamboat that takes one
round by the open sea, and up through the
mouth of the St. John's River, to Jacksonville.
Any one who has come to see scenery should
choose this route. The entrance of the St.
John's from the ocean is one of the most singular and impressive passages of scenery that we

ever passed through : in fine weather the sight
is magnificent.

Besides this, a smaller boat takes passengers
to Jacksonville by what is called the inside passage, — a circuitous course through the network
of islands that lines the shore. This course also
offers a great deal of curious interest to one new
to Southern scenery, and has attractions for
those who dread the sea. By any of these
courses Florida may be gained in a few hours
or days, more or less, from Savannah.

A FLOWERY JANUARY IN FLORIDA.

MANDARIN, FLA., Jan. 24, 1872.

YES, it is done. The winter is over and past, and " the time of the singing of birds is come." They are at it beak and claw, — the red-birds, and the cat-birds, and the chattering jays, and the twittering sparrows, busy and funny and bright. Down in the swamp-land fronting our cottage, four calla-lily buds are just unfolding themselves ; and in the little garden-plat at one side stand rose-geraniums and camellias, white and pink, just unfolding.

Right opposite to the window, through which the morning sun is pouring, stands a stately orange-tree, thirty feet high, with spreading, graceful top, and varnished green leaves, full of golden fruit. These are the veritable golden apples of the Hesperides, — the apples that Atalanta threw in the famous race ; and they are good enough to be run after. The things that fill the New-York market, called by courtesy "oranges," — pithy, wilted, and sour, — have not even a suggestion of what those golden balls are that weigh down the great glossy green branches of yonder tree. At the tree's foot, Aunt Katy does her weekly washing in the open air the winter through. We have been putting our tape-measure about it, and find it forty-three inches in girth ; and for shapely beauty it has no equal. It gives one a sort of heart-thrill of possession to say of such beauty, "It is mine." No wonder the Scripture says, " He that is so impoverished that he hath

2

no oblation chooseth a tree that will not rot."
The orange-tree is, in our view, the best worthy
to represent the tree of life of any that grows
on our earth.   It is the fairest, the noblest, the
most generous, it is the most upspringing and
abundant, of all trees which the Lord God
caused to grow eastward in Eden.   Its wood is
white and hard and tough, fit to sustain the
immense weight of its fruitage.   Real good ripe
oranges are very heavy ; and the generosity of
the tree inclines it to fruit in clusters.   We
counted, the other day, a cluster of eighteen,
hanging low, and weighing down the limb.

But this large orange-tree, and many larger
than this, which are parts of one orchard, are
comparatively recent growths.   In 1835, every
one of them was killed even with the ground.
Then they started up with the genuine pluck of
a true-born orange-tree, which never says die,
and began to grow again.   Nobody pruned them,

or helped them, or cared much about them any
way ; and you can see trees that have grown up
in four, five, and six trunks,—just as the suckers
sprung up from the roots. Then, when they had
made some progress, came the orange-insect, and
nearly killed them down again. The owners of
the land, discouraged, broke down the fences,
and moved off; and for a while the land was
left an open common, where wild cattle browsed,
and rubbed themselves on the trees. But still,
in spite of all, they have held on their way
rejoicing, till now they are the beautiful creatures they are. Truly we may call them trees
of the Lord, full of sap and greenness ; full of
lessons of perseverance to us who get frosted
down and cut off, time and time again, in our
lives. Let us hope in the Lord, and be up and
at it again.

It is certainly quite necessary to have some
such example before our eyes in struggling to

found a colony here. We had such a hard time getting our church and schoolhouse!—for in these primitive regions one building must do for both. There were infinite negotiations and cases to go through before a site could be bought with a clear title; and the Freedman's Bureau would put us up a building where school could be taught on week-days, and worship held on Sundays: but at last it was done; and a neat, pleasant little place it was.

We had a little Mason and Hamlin missionary organ, which we used to carry over on Sundays, and a cloth, which converted the master's desk of week-days into the minister's pulpit; and as we had minister, organist, and choir all in our own family, we were sure of them at all events; and finally a good congregation was being gathered. On week-days a school for whites and blacks was taught, until the mismanagement of the school-fund had used up the sum devoted to common schools, and left us without a teacher for a year. But this fall our friend Mr. D., who had accepted the situation of county overseer of schools, had just completed arrangements to open again both the white and the black schools, when, lo! in one night our poor little schoolhouse was burned to the ground, with our Mason and Hamlin organ in it. Latterly it had been found inconvenient to carry it backward and forward; and so it had been left, locked in a closet, and met a fiery doom. We do not suppose any malicious incendiarism. There appears evidence that some strolling loafers had gotten in to spend the night, and probably been careless of their fire. The southern pine is inflammable as so much pitch, and will almost light with the scratch of a match. Well, all we had to do was to imitate the pluck of the orange-trees, which we immediately did. Our neighborhood had

increased by three or four families; and a meeting was immediately held, and each one pledged
himself to raise a certain sum. We feel the
want of it more for the schoolhouse than even
for the church. We go on with our Sunday
services at each other's houses; but alas for
the poor children, black and white, growing up
so fast, who have been kept out of school now a
year, and who are losing these best months for
study! To see people who are willing and
anxious to be taught growing up in ignorance
is the sorest sight that can afflict one; and we
count the days until we shall have our church
and schoolhouse again. But, meanwhile, Mandarin presents to our eyes a marvellously improved aspect. Two or three large, handsome
houses are built up in our immediate neighborhood. Your old collaborator of " The Christian
Union" has a most fascinating place a short distance from us, commanding a noble sweep of

view up and down the river. On our right hand, two gentlemen from Newark have taken each a lot ; and the gables of the house of one of them overlook the orange-trees bravely from the river.

This southern pine, unpainted, makes a rich, soft color for a house. Being merely oiled, it turns a soft golden brown, which harmonizes charmingly with the landscape.

How cold is it here? We ask ourselves, a dozen times a day, "What season is it?" We say, "This spring," "This summer," and speak of our Northern life as "last winter." There are cold nights, and, occasionally, white frosts : but the degree of cold may be judged from the fact that the Calla Ethiopica goes on budding and blossoming out of doors; that La Marque roses have not lost their leaves, and have long, young shoots on them ; and that our hand-maiden, a pretty, young mulattress, occasionally brings to us a whole dish of roses and buds which her devoted has brought her from some back cottage in the pine-woods. We have also eaten the last *fresh* tomatoes from the old vines since we came; but a pretty severe frost has nipped them, as well as cut off a promising lot of young peas just coming into pod. But the pea-vines will still grow along, and we shall have others soon.

We eat radishes out of the ground, and lettuce, now and then, a little nipped by the frost; and we get long sprays of yellow jessamine, just beginning to blossom in the woods.

Yes, it is spring; though still it is cold enough to make our good bright fire a rallying-point to the family. It is good to keep fire in a country where it is considered a great point to get rid of wood. One piles and heaps up with a genial cheer when one thinks, "The more you burn, the better." It only costs what you pay for cutting and hauling. We begin to find our usual number of letters, wanting to know all this, that, and the other, about Florida. All in good time, friends. Come down here once, and use your own eyes, and you will know more than we can teach you. Till when, adieu.

THE WRONG SIDE OF THE TAPESTRY.

IT is not to be denied that full half of the tourists and travellers that come to Florida return intensely disappointed, and even disgusted. Why? Evidently because Florida, like a piece of embroidery, has two sides to it, — one side all tag-rag and thrums, without order or position; and the other side showing flowers and arabesques and brilliant coloring. Both these sides exist. Both are undeniable, un-disputed facts, not only in the case of Florida, but of every place and thing under the sun. There

is a right side and a wrong side to every
thing.

Now, tourists and travellers generally come
with their heads full of certain romantic ideas
of waving palms, orange-groves, flowers, and
fruit, all bursting forth in tropical abundance ;
and, in consequence, they go through Florida
with disappointment at every step.   If the banks
of the St. John's were covered with orange-
groves, if they blossomed every month in the
year, if they were always loaded with fruit, if
pine-apples and bananas grew wild, if the flowers
hung in festoons from tree to tree, if the ground
were enamelled with them all winter long, so that
you saw nothing else, then they would begin to
be satisfied.

But, in point of fact, they find, in approaching
Florida, a dead sandy level, with patches behind them of rough coarse grass, and tall pine-
trees, whose tops are so far in the air that they

seem to cast no shade, and a little scrubby under-brush. The few houses to be seen along the railroad are the forlornest of huts. The cattle that stray about are thin and poverty-stricken, and look as if they were in the last tottering stages of starvation.

Then, again, winter, in a semi-tropical region, has a peculiar desolate untidiness, from the fact that there is none of that clearing of the trees and shrubs which the sharp frosts of the northern regions occasion. Here the leaves, many of them, though they have lost their beauty, spent their strength, and run their course, do not fall thoroughly and cleanly, but hang ·on in ragged patches, waiting to be pushed off by the swelling buds of next year. In New England, Nature is an up-and-down, smart, decisive house-mother, that has her times and seasons, and brings up her ends of life with a positive jerk. She will have no shilly-shally.

When her time comes, she clears off the gardens and forests thoroughly and once for all, and they are clean. Then she freezes the ground solid as iron ; and then she covers all up with a nice pure winding-sheet of snow, and seals matters up as a good housewife does her jelly tumblers under white-paper covers. There you are fast and cleanly. If you have not got ready for it, so much the worse for you! If your tender roots are not taken up, your cellar banked, your doors listed, she can't help it : it's your own lookout, not hers.

But Nature down here is an easy, demoralized, indulgent old grandmother, who has no particular time for any thing, and does every thing when she happens to feel like it. "Is it winter, or isn't it?" is the question that is likely often to occur in the settling month of December, when everybody up North has put away summer clothes, and put all their establishments under winter-orders.

Consequently, on arriving in mid-winter time, the first thing that strikes the eye is the ragged, untidy look of the foliage and shrubbery. About one-third of the trees are deciduous, and stand entirely bare of leaves. The rest are evergreen, which by this time, having come through the fierce heats of summer, have acquired a seared and dusky hue, different from the vivid brightness of early spring. In the garden you see all the half-and-half proceedings which mark the indefinite boundaries of the season. The rose-bushes have lost about half their green leaves. Some varieties, however, in this climate, seem to be partly evergreen. The La Marque and the crimson rose, sometimes called Louis Philippe, seem to keep their last year's foliage till spring pushes it off with new leaves.

Once in a while, however, Nature, like a grandmother in a fret, comes down on you with a most unexpected snub. You have a cold spell, — an actual frost. During the five years in which we have made this our winter residence, there have twice been frosts severe enough to spoil the orange-crop, though not materially injuring the trees.

This present winter has been generally a colder one than usual ; but there have been no hurtful frosts. But one great cause of disgust and provocation of tourists in Florida is the occurrence of these " cold snaps." It is really amusing to see how people accustomed to the tight freezes, the drifting snow wreaths, the stinging rain, hail, and snow, of the Northern winter, will *take on* when the thermometer goes down to 30° or 32°, and a white frost is seen out of doors. They are perfectly outraged. "*Such* weather ! If this is your Florida winter, deliver me!" All the while they could walk out any day into the woods, as we have done, and gather

eight or ten varieties of flowers blooming in the
open air, and eat radishes and lettuce and peas
grown in the garden.

Well, it is to be confessed that the cold of
warm climates always has a peculiarly aggravat-
ing effect on the mind. A warm region is just
like some people who get such a character for
good temper, that they never can indulge themselves even in an earnest disclaimer without
everybody crying out upon them, " What puts
you in such a passion ? " &c. So Nature, if she
generally sets up for amiability during the winter months, cannot be allowed a little tiff now
and then, a white frost, a cold rain-storm, without being considered a monster.

It is to be confessed that the chill of warm
climates, when they are chilly, is peculiar ; and
travellers should prepare for it, not only in mind,
but in wardrobe, by carrying a plenty of warm
clothing, and, above all, an inestimable India-

rubber bottle, which they can fill with hot water to dissipate the chill at night. An experience of four winters leads us to keep on about the usual winter clothing until March or April. The first day after our arrival, to be sure, we put away all our furs as things of the past; but we keep abundance of warm shawls, and, above all, wear the usual flannels till late in the spring.

Invalids seeking a home here should be particularly careful to secure rooms in which there can be a fire. It is quite as necessary as at the North; and, with this comfort, the cold spells, few in number as they are, can be easily passed by.

Our great feature in the Northern landscape, which one never fails to miss and regret here, is the grass. The *nakedness* of the land is an expression that often comes over one. The peculiar sandy soil is very difficult to arrange in any tidy fashion. You cannot make beds or alleys of it: it all runs together like a place

3

where hens have been scratching ; and consequently it is the most difficult thing in the
world to have ornamental grounds.

At the North, the process of making a new
place appear neat and inviting is very rapid.
One season of grass-seed, and the thing is done.
Here, however, it is the most difficult thing in
the world to get turf of any sort to growing.
The Bermuda grass, and a certain coarse, broad-
leafed turf, are the only kind that can stand the
summer heat ; and these never have the beauty
of well-ordered Northern grass.

Now, we have spent anxious hours and much
labor over a little plot in our back-yard, which
we seeded with white clover, and which, for a
time, was green and lovely to behold ; but, alas !
the Scripture was too strikingly verified :
"When the sun shineth on it with a burning
heat, it withereth the grass, and the grace of
the fashion of it perisheth."

The fact is, that people cannot come to heartily like Florida till they *accept* certain deficiencies as the necessary shadow to certain excellences. If you want to live in an orange-orchard, you must give up wanting to live surrounded by green grass. When we get to the new heaven and the new earth, then we shall have it all right. There we shall have a climate at once cool and bracing, yet hot enough to mature oranges and pine-apples. Our trees of life shall bear twelve manner of fruit, and yield a new one every month. Out of juicy meadows green as emerald, enamelled with every kind of flower, shall grow our golden orange-trees, blossoming and fruiting together as now they do. There shall be no mosquitoes, or gnats, or black-flies, or snakes ; and, best of all, there shall be no fretful people. Everybody shall be like a well-tuned instrument, all sounding in accord, and never a semitone out of the way.

Meanwhile, we caution everybody coming to
Florida, Don't hope for too much.   Because you
hear that roses and callas blossom in the open
air all winter, and flowers abound in the woods,
don't expect to find an eternal summer.   Prepare
yourself to see a great deal that looks rough
and desolate and coarse ; prepare yourself for
some chilly days and nights ; and, whatever else
you neglect to bring with you, bring the resolu-
tion, strong and solid, always to make the best
of things.

For ourselves, we are getting reconciled to a
sort of tumble-down, wild, picnicky kind of life,
— this general happy-go-luckiness which Florida
inculcates.   If we painted her, we should not
represent her as a neat, trim damsel, with
starched linen cuffs and collar : she would be
a brunette, dark but comely, with gorgeous
tissues, a general disarray and dazzle, and with
a sort of jolly untidiness, free, easy, and joyous.

The great charm, after all, of this life, is its outdoorness. To be able to spend your winter out of doors, even though some days be cold ; to be able to sit with windows open ; to hear birds daily ; to eat fruit from trees, and pick flowers from hedges, all winter long, — is about the whole of the story. This you can do ; and this is why Florida is life and health to the invalid.

We get every year quantities of letters from persons of small fortunes, asking our advice whether they had better move to Florida. For our part, we never advise people to *move* anywhere. As a general rule, it is the person who feels the inconveniences of a present position, so as to want to move, who will feel the inconvenience of a future one. Florida has a lovely winter ; but it has also three formidable summer months, July, August, and September, when the heat is excessive, and the liabilities of new settlers to sickness so great, that we should never wish to take the responsibility of bringing anybody here. It is true that a very comfortable number of people do live through them; but still it is not a joke, by any means, to move to a new country. The first colony in New England lost just half its members in the first six months. The rich bottom-lands around Cincinnati proved graves to many a family before they were brought under cultivation.

But Florida is peculiarly adapted to the needs of people who can afford two houses, and want a refuge from the drain that winter makes on the health. As people now have summer-houses at Nahant or Rye, so they might, at a small expense, have winter-houses in Florida, and come here and be at home. That is the great charm, — to be at home. A house here can be simple and inexpensive, and yet very charming. Already, around us a pretty group of winter-houses is rising : and we look forward to the time when there shall be many more ; when, all along the shore of the St. John's, cottages and villas shall look out from the green trees.

A LETTER TO THE GIRLS.

YES, the girls! Let me see: who are they? I mean *you*, Nellie, and Mary, and Emily, and Charlotte, and Gracie, and Susie, and Carry, and Kitty, and you of every pretty name, my charming little Pussy Willow friends! Dear souls all, I bless your bright eyes, and fancy you about me as a sort of inspiration to my writing. I could wish you were every one here. Don't you wish that "The Arabian Nights" were true? and that there were really little square bits of enchanted carpet, on which one has only to sit down and pronounce two cabalistic words, and away one goes through the air, sailing off on visits? Then, girls, wouldn't we have a nice wide bit of carpet? and wouldn't we have the whole bright flock of you come fluttering down together to play croquet with us under the orange-trees this afternoon? And, while you were waiting for your turns to come, you should reach up and pull down a bough, and help yourselves to oranges; or you should join a party now going out into the pine-woods to gather yellow jessamine. To-day is mail-day; and, as the yellow jessamine is in all its glory, the girls here are sending little boxes of it North to their various friends through the mail. They have just been bringing in long wreaths and clusters of it for me to look at, and are consulting how to pack it. Then this afternoon, when we have done croquet, it is proposed that we form a party to visit Aunt Katy, who lives about two miles away in the pine-woods, "over on Julington" as the people here say. " On Julington" means on a branch of the St. John's named Julington Creek, although it is as wide as the Connecticut River at Hartford. We put the oldest mule to an old wagon, and walk and ride alternately ; some of us riding one way, and some the other.

The old mule, named Fly, is a worn-out, ancient patriarch, who, having worked all his days without seeing any particular use in it, is now getting rather misanthropic in his old age, and obstinately determined not to put one foot before the other one bit faster than he is actually forced to do. Only the most vigorous urging can get him to step out of a walk, although we are told that the rogue has a very fair trot at his command. If any of the darky tribe are behind him, he never thinks of doing any thing but pricking up his ears, and trotting at a decent pace ; but, when only girls and women are to the fore, down flop his ears, down goes his head, and he creeps obstinately along in the afore-mentioned contemplative manner, looking, for all the world, like a very rough, dilapidated old hair-trunk in a state of locomotion.

Well, I don't blame him, poor brute! Life, I suppose, is as much a mystery to him as to the philosophers; and he has never been able to settle what it is all about, this fuss of being harnessed periodically to impertinent carts, and driven here and there, for no valuable purpose that he can see.

Such as he is, Fly is the absolute property of the girls and women, being past farm-work ; and though he never willingly does any thing but walk, yet his walk is considerably faster than that of even the most agile of us, and he is by many degrees better than nothing. He is admitted on all hands to be a *safe* beast, and will certainly never run away with any of us.

As to the choice of excursions, there are several, — one to our neighbor Bowens to see sugar-making, where we can watch the whole process, from the grinding of the cane through the various vats and boilers, till at last we see the perfected sugar in fine, bright, straw-colored crystals in the sugar-house. We are hospitably treated to saucers of lovely, amber-colored sirup just on the point of crystallization, — liquid sugar-candy, — which, of course, we do not turn away from. Then, again, we can go down the banks of the river to where our neighbor Duncan has cleared up a little spot in what used to be virgin forest, and where now a cosey little cottage is beginning to peep through its many windows upon the river-view. Here a bright little baby — a real little Florida flower — has lately opened a pair of lovely eyes, and is growing daily in grace and favor. In front of this cottage, spared from the forest, are three great stately magnolias, such trees as you never saw. Their leaves resemble those of the India-rubber tree, — large, and of a glossy, varnished green. They are evergreen, and in May are covered with great white blossoms, something like pond-lilies, and with very much the same odor. The trees at the North called magnolias give no idea whatever of what these are. They are giants among flowers; seem worthy to be trees of heaven.

Then there are all sorts of things to be got out of the woods. There are palmetto-leaves to be pressed and dried, and made into fans; there is the long wire-grass, which can be sewed into mats, baskets, and various little fancy articles, by busy fingers. Every day brings something to explore the woods for: not a day in winter passes that you cannot bring home a reasonable little nosegay of flowers. Many of the flowers here do not have their seasons, but seem to bloom the year round : so that, all the time, you are sure of finding something. The woods now are full of bright, delicate ferns that no frosts have touched, and that spring and grow perennially. The book of Nature here is never shut and clasped with ice and snow as at the North ; and, of course, we spend about half our time in the open air.

The last sensation of our circle is our red-bird. We do not approve of putting free birds in cages ; but Aunt Katy brought to one of our party such a beautiful fellow, so brilliant a red, with such a smart, black crest on his head, and such a long, flashing red tail, that we couldn't resist the desire to keep him a little while, just to look at him. Aunt Katy insisted that he wouldn't take it to heart ; that he would be tame in a few days, and eat out of our hands : in short, she insisted that he would consider himself a fortunate bird to belong to us.

Aunt Katy, you must know, is a nice old lady We use that term with a meaning; for, though "black as the tents of Kedar," she is a perfect lady in her manners: she was born and brought up, and has always lived, in this neighborhood, and knows every bird in the forest as familiarly as if they were all her own chickens; and she has great skill in getting them to come to her to be caught.

Well, our red-bird was named Phœbus, of a kind that Audubon calls a cardinal-grossbeak; and a fine, large, roomy cage was got down for him, which was of old tenanted by a very merry and rackety cat-bird; and then the question arose, "What shall we do with him?" For you see, girls, having a soft place in our heart for all pets, instead of drowning some of our kittens in the fall, as reasonable people should, we were seduced by their gambols and their prettiness to let them all grow up together; and the result is,

that we have now in our domestic retinue four
adult cats of most formidable proportions.
" These be the generations " of our cats : first,
Liz, the mother; second, Peter, her oldest son;
third, Anna and Lucinda, her daughters. Peter
is a particularly martial, combative, obnoxious
beast, very fluffy and fussy, with great, full-
moon, yellow eyes, and a most resounding,
sonorous voice. There is an immense deal of
cat in Peter. He is concentrated cathood, a
nugget of pure cat ; and in fact we are all a
little in awe of him. He rules his mother and
sisters as if he had never heard of Susan
Anthony and Mrs. Stanton. Liz, Anna, and
Lucinda are also wonderfully-well-developed cats,
with capital stomachs. Now comes the problem : the moment the red-bird was let into his
cage, there was an instant whisk of tails, and a
glare of great yellow eyes, and a sharpening of
eye-teeth, that marked a situation. The Scrip

ture tells us a time is coming when the lion shall lie down with the lamb; but that time hasn't come in Florida. Peter is a regular heathen, and hasn't the remotest idea of the millennium. He has much of the lion in him; but he never could lie down peaceably with the lamb, unless indeed the lamb were inside of him, when he would sleep upon him without a twinge of conscience. Unmistakably we could see in his eyes that he considered Phœbus as caught for his breakfast; and he sat licking his chops inquiringly, as who should ask, "When will the cloth be laid, and things be ready?"

Now, the party to whom the red-bird was given is also the patron-saint, the "guide, philosopher, and friend," of the cats. It is she who examines the plates after each meal, and treasures fragments, which she cuts up and prepares for their repast with commendable regularity. It is she who presides and keeps order at cat-meals ; and forasmuch as Peter, on account of his masculine strength and rapacity, is apt to get the better of his mother and sisters, she picks him up, and bears him growling from the board, when he has demolished his own portion, and is proceeding to eat up theirs.

Imagine, now, the cares of a woman with four cats and a bird on her mind! Phœbus had to be carefully pinned up in a blanket the first night ; then the cage was swung by strong cords from the roof of the veranda. The next morning, Peter was found perched on top of it, glaring fiendishly. The cage was moved along ; and Peter scaled a pillar, and stationed himself at the side. To be sure, he couldn't get the bird, as the slats were too close for his paw to go through ; but poor Phœbus seemed wild with terror. Was it for this he left his native wilds, — to be exposed in a prison to glaring, wild-eyed hyenas and tigers ?

The cats were admonished, chastised, "scat"-ed, through all the moods and tenses; though their patroness still serves out their commons regularly, determined that they shall not have the apology of empty stomachs. Phœbus is evidently a philosopher, — a bird of strong sense. Having found, after two or three days' trial, that the cats can't get him; having clusters of the most delicious rice dangling from the roof of his cage, and fine crisp lettuce verdantly inviting through the bars, — he seems to have accepted the situation; and, when nobody is in the veranda, he uplifts his voice in song. "What cheer! what cheer!" he says, together with many little twitters and gurgles for which we have no musical notes. Aunt Katy promises to bring him a little wife before long; and, if that be given him, what shall hinder him from being happy? As April comes in, they shall build their nest in the cage, and give us a flock of little red-birds.

Well, girls, we are making a long letter; and this must do for this week.

A WATER-COACH, AND A RIDE IN IT.

MONDAY, Feb. 26, 1872.

DEAR girls, wouldn't you like to get into that little white yacht that lies dancing and courtesying on the blue waters of the St. John's this pleasant Monday morning?

It is a day of days. Spring has come down with all her smiles and roses in one hour. The great blue sheet of water shimmers and glitters like so much liquid *lapis lazuli;* and now the word comes in from our neighbor, the owner of the pleasure-yacht, "Wouldn't you like to go sailing?"

Of course we should! That is exactly what we *do* want. And forthwith there is a running and a mustering of the clans, and a flapping of broad palmetto-hats; and parties from all the three houses file down, and present themselves as candidates for pleasure. A great basket of oranges is hoisted in, and the white sails spread; and with "Youth at the prow, and Pleasure at the helm," away we go, the breezes blowing manfully at our sails. The river is about five miles from shore to shore, and we have known it of old for a most enticing and tricksy customer. It gently wooes and seduces you; it starts you out with all manner of zephyrs, until you get into the very middle, two miles from land on either side, when down goes your limp sail, and the breeze is off on some other errand,

and you are left to your reflections. Not immediately did this happen to us, however ; though, when we came to the middle of the river, our course was slow enough to give plenty of opportunity to discuss the basket of oranges. We settle it among us that we will cross to Doctor's Lake. This name is given to a wide bayou which the river makes, running up into the forest for a track of about nine miles. It is a famous fishing and hunting region, and a favorite and chosen abode of the alligators. At the farther end of it are said to be swamps where they have their lairs, and lay their eggs, and hatch out charming young alligators. Just at the opening where the river puts into this lake are the nets of the shad-fishers, who supply the Jacksonville market with that delicious article. We are minded to go over and fill our provision-baskets before they go.

Now we near the opposite shore of the river.

We see the great tuft of Spanish oaks which
marks the house of the old Macintosh plantation, once the palmiest in Florida. This de-
mesne had nine thousand acres of land, includ-
ing in it the Doctor's Lake and the islands
therein, with all the store of swamps and forests
and alligators' nests, wild-orange groves, and palmetto-jungles. It was a sort of pride of terri-
tory that animated these old aboriginal planters;
for, of the whole nine thousand acres which
formed the estate, only about five hundred ever
were cleared, and subject to cultivation. One of
these days we are projecting to spend a day picnicking on this old plantation, now deserted and
decaying; and then we can tell you many curious
things in its history. But now we are coming
close alongside the shad-nets. We find no fishermen to traffic with. Discerning a rude hut on
the opposite side of the bayou, we make for that,
expecting there to find them. We hail a boy
who lies idly in a boat by the shore.

"Halloo, my fine fellow! Can you tell us where the people are that tend that net?"

"Don't know," is the reply that comes over the water.

"Can you sell us any fish?"

"Got a couple o' trout."

"Bring 'em along." And away we go, rippling before the breeze; while the boy, with the graceful deliberation which marks the movements of the native population, prepares to come after us.

"I don't believe he understood," said one.

"Oh, yes! He's only taking his time, as they all do down here. He'll be along in the course of the forenoon."

At last he comes alongside, and shows a couple of great black-looking, goggle-eyed fish, which look more like incipient cod or haddock than trout. Such as they are, however, we conclude a bargain for them; and away goes our boy with fifty cents in his pocket. What he can want of fifty cents in a hut on the other side of Doctor's Lake is a question. Can he trade with alligators? But he has a boat; and we foresee that that boat will make a voyage across to the grocery on the opposite point, where whiskey, pork, and flour are sold. Meanwhile we looked at the little rude hut again. It was Monday morning; and a string of clothes was fluttering on a line, and a good many little garments among them. There is a mother, then, and a family of children growing up. We noticed the sheen of three or four orange-trees, probably wild ones, about the house. Now we go rippling up the bayou, close along by the shore. The land is swampy, and the forests glister with the shining, varnished leaves of the magnolias; and we saw far within the waving green fans of the swamp-palmetto. The gum-trees and water-oaks were just bursting into leaf with that dazzling green of early spring which is almost metallic in brilliancy. The maples were throwing out blood-red keys, — larger and higher-colored than the maples of the North. There is a whir of wings ; and along the opposite shore of the bayou the wild-ducks file in long platoons. Now and then a water-turkey, with his long neck and legs, varies the scene. There swoops down a fish-hawk ; and we see him bearing aloft a silvery fish, wriggling and twisting in his grasp. We were struck with the similarity of our tastes. He was fond of shad: so were we. He had a wriggling fish in his claws ; and we had a couple flapping and bouncing in the basket, over which we were gloating. There was but one point of difference. He, undoubtedly, would eat his fish raw ; whereas we were planning to have ours cut in slices, and fried with salt pork. Otherwise the fish-hawk and we were out on the same errand, with the same results.

Yet at first view, I must confess, when we saw him rise with a wriggling fish in his claws, he struck us as a monster. It seemed a savage proceeding, and we pitied the struggling fish, while ours were yet flapping in the basket. This eating-business is far from pleasant to contemplate. Every thing seems to be in for it. It is "catch who catch can" through all the animal kingdom till it comes up to man; and he eats the whole, choosing or refusing as suits his taste. One wonders why there was not a superior order of beings made to eat us. Mosquitoes and black-flies get now and then a nip, to be sure; but there is nobody provided to make a square meal of us, as we do on a wild turkey, for example. But speaking of eating, and discussing fried fish and salt pork, aroused harrowing reflections in our company. We found ourselves at one o'clock in the middle of Doctor's Lake, with the dinner-shore at least five miles away ; and it was agreed, *nem. con.*, that it was time to put about. The fish-hawk had suggested dinner-time.

And now came the beauty of the proceeding. We drove merrily out of Doctor's Lake into the beautiful blue middle of the St. John's : and there the zephyrs gayly whispered, "Good-by, friends ; and, when you get ashore, let us know." The river was like a molten looking-glass, the sun staring steadfastly down. There is nothing for it but to get out the oars, and pull strong and steady ; and so we do. It is the old trick of this St John's, whereby muscular development is promoted. First two gentlemen row ; then a lady takes one oar, and we work our way along to the shore ; but it is full four o'clock before we get there.

As we approach, we pass brisk little nine-year-old Daisy, who is out alone in her boat, with her doll-carriage and doll. She has been rowing down to make a morning call on Bessie, and is now returning. Off on the end of the wharf we see the whole family watching for our return. The Professor's white beard and red fez cap make a striking point in the tableau. Our little friend Bob, and even baby and mamma, are on the point of observation. It is past four o'clock, dinner long over; and they have all been wondering what has got us. We walk straight up to the house, with but one idea, — dinner. We cease to blame the fish-hawk, being in a condition fully to enter into his feelings : a little more, and we could eat fish as he does, — without roasting. Doubtless he and Mrs. Fish-hawk, and the little Fish-hawks, may have been discussing us over their savory meal ; but we find little to say till dinner is despatched.

The last hour on board the boat had been devoted to a course of reflections on our folly in starting out without luncheon, and to planning a more advised excursion up Julington Creek with all the proper paraphernalia ; viz., a kerosene-stove for making coffee, an embankment of ham-sandwiches, diversified with cakes, crackers, and cheese. This, it is understood, is to come off to-morrow morning.

Tuesday Morning, Feb. 27. —- Such was to have been my programme ; but, alas ! this morning, though the day rose bright and clear, there was not a breath of wind. The river has looked all day like a sheet of glass. There is a drowsy, hazy calm over every thing. All our windows and doors are open ; and every sound seems to be ringingly distinct. The chatter and laughing of the children, (God bless 'em !) who are all day long frolicking on the end of the wharf, or rowing about in the boats ; the leisurely chip, chip, of the men who are busy in mending the steamboat wharf; the hammer of the carpenters on the yet unfinished part of our neighbor's house ; the scream of the jays in the orange-trees, — all blend in a sort of dreamy indistinctness.

To-day is one of the two red-letter days of our week, — the day of the arrival of the mail. You who have a driblet two or three times a day from the mail cannot conceive the interest that gathers around these two weekly arrivals. The whole forenoon is taken up with it. We sit on the veranda, and watch the mail-boat far down the river, — a mere white speck as she passes through the wooded opening above Jacksonville. She grows larger and larger as she comes sailing up like a great white stately swan, first on the farther side of the river till she comes to Reed's Landing ; and then, turning her white breast full toward Mandarin Wharf, she comes ploughing across, freighted with all our hopes and fears. Then follows the rush for our mail ; then the distribution : after which all depart to their several apartments with their letters.

Then follow readings to each other, general tidings and greetings ; and when the letters are all read twice over, and thoroughly discussed, come the papers. Tuesday is "The Christian Union" day, as well as the day for about a dozen other papers ; and the Professor is seen henceforward with bursting pockets, like a very large carnation bursting its calyx. He is a walking mass of papers.

The afternoon has been devoted to reflection, gossiping, and various expeditions. B. and G. have gone boating with Mr. —— ; and come home, on the edge of the evening, with the animating news that they have seen the two first alligators of the season. That shows that warm weather is to be expected ; for your alligator is a delicate beast, and never comes out when there is the least danger of catching cold. Another party have been driving "Fly" through the woods to Julington Creek, and come back reporting that they have seen an owl. The Professor gives report of having seen two veritable wild-turkeys and a blue crane, — news which touches us all tenderly ; for we have as yet had not a turkey to our festive board. We ourselves have been having a quiet game of croquet out under the orange-trees, playing till we could see the wickets no longer. So goes our day, — breezy, open-aired, and full of variety. Your world, Mr. Union, is seen in perspective, far off and hazy, like the opposite shores of the river. Nevertheless, this is the place to *read* papers and books ; for every thing that sweeps into this quiet bay is long and quietly considered. We shall have something anon to say as to how you all look in the blue perspective of distance.

Meanwhile, we must tell the girls that Phœbus has wholly accommodated himself to his situation, and wakes us, mornings, with his singing. "What cheer ! what cheer !" he says.

Whether he alludes to the four cats, or to his large cage, or to his own internal determination, like Mark Tapley, to be jolly, isn't evident.

Last week, Aunt Katy brought a mate for him, which was christened Luna. She was a pretty creature, smaller, less brilliant, but gracefully shaped, and with a nice crest on her head. We regret to say that she lived only a few hours, being found dead in the cage in the morning. A day or two since, great sympathy was expressed for Phœbus, in view of the matrimonial happiness of a pair of red-birds who came to survey our yellow jessamine with a view to setting up housekeeping there. Would not the view of freedom and wedded joys depress his spirits? Not a bit of it. He is evidently cut out for a jolly bachelor; and, as long as he has fine chambers and a plenty of rough rice, what cares he for family life? The heartless fellow piped up, "What cheer! what cheer!" the very day that he got his cage to himself. Is this peculiar? A lady at our table has stated it as a universal fact, that, as soon as a man's wife dies, he immediately gets a new suit of clothes. Well, why shouldn't he? Nothing conduces more to cheerfulness. On the whole, we think Phœbus is a pattern bird.

P. S. — Ask the author of "My Summer in a Garden" if he can't condense his account of "Calvin's" virtues into a tract, to be distributed among our cats. Peter is such a hardened sinner, a little Calvinism might operate well on him.

PICNICKING UP JULINGTON.

MANDARIN, FLA., Feb. 29, 1872.

THIS twenty-ninth day of February is a day made on purpose for a fishing-party. A day that comes only once in four years certainly ought to be good for something; and this is as good a day for picnicking up Julington as if it had been bespoken four years ahead. A bright sun, a blue sky, a fresh, strong breeze upon the water, — these are Nature's contributions. Art contributes two

trim little white yachts, " The Nelly " and " The
Bessie," and three row-boats. Down we all
troop to the landing with our luncheon-baskets,
kerosene-stove, tea-kettle, and coffee-pot, baskets
of oranges, and fishing-reels.

Out flutter the sails, and away we go. No danger to-day of being left in the lurch in the middle
of the river. There is all the breeze one wants,
and a little more than the timorous love ; and
we go rippling and racing through the water in
merry style. The spray flies, so that we need
our water-proofs and blankets; but the more the
merrier. We sweep gallantly first by the cottage of your whilom editor in " The Union," and
get a friendly salute; and then flutter by D——'s
cottage, and wave our handkerchiefs, and get
salutes in return. Now we round the point, and
Julington opens her wide blue arms to receive us.
We pass by Neighbor H——'s, and again wave
our handkerchiefs, and get answering salutes.

We run up to the wharf to secure another boat and oarsman in the person of Neighbor P——, and away we fly up Julington. A creek it is called, but fully as wide as the Connecticut at Hartford, and wooded to the water on either side by these glorious Florida forests.

It is a late, backward spring for Florida ; and so these forests are behindhand with their foliage : yet so largely do they consist of bright polished evergreen trees, that the eye scarcely feels the need of the deciduous foliage on which the bright misty green of spring lies like an uncertain vapor. There is a large admixture in the picture of the cool tints of the gray moss, which drapes every tree, and hangs in long pendent streamers waving in the wind. The shores of the creek now begin to be lined on either side with tracts of a water-lily which the natives call bonnets. The blossom is like that of our yellow pond-lily ; but the leaves are very

broad and beautiful as they float like green
islands on the blue waters. Here and there,
even in the centre of the creek, are patches of
them intermingled with quantities of the water-
lettuce, — a floating plant which abounds in
these tracts. Along the edges of these water-lily
patches are the favorite haunts of the fish, who
delight to find shelter among the green leaves.
So the yachts come to anchor ; and the party
divides into the three row-boats, and prepares to
proceed to business.

We have some bustle in distributing our stove
and tea-kettle and lunch-baskets to the different
boats, as we are to row far up stream, and, when
we have caught our dinner, land, and cook it.   I
sit in the bow, and, being good for nothing in
the fishing-line, make myself of service by
holding the French coffee-pot in my lap. The
tea-kettle being at my feet on one side, the stove
on the other, and the luncheon-basket in full

view in front, I consider myself as, in a sense, at housekeeping. Meanwhile the fishing-reels are produced, the lines thrown ; and the professional fishermen and fisherwomen become all absorbed in their business. We row slowly along the bobbing, undulating field of broad green bonnet-leaves, and I deliver myself to speculations on Nature. The roots of these water-lilies, of the size of a man's arm, often lie floating for yards on the surface, and, with their scaly joints, look like black serpents. The ribbed and shining leaves, as they float out upon the water, are very graceful. One is struck with a general similarity in the plant and animal growths in these regions : the element of grotesqueness seems largely to enter into it. Roots of plants become scaly, contorted, and lie in convolutions like the coils of a serpent. Such are the palmetto-shrubs, whose roots lie in scaly folds along the ground, catching into the

earth by strong rootlets, and then rising up here
and there into tall, waving green fans, whose
graceful beauty in the depths of these forests
one is never tired of admiring. Amid this
serpent-like and convoluted jungle of scaly
roots, how natural to find the scaly alligator,
looking like an animated form of the grotesque
vegetable world around! Sluggish, unwieldy, he
seems a half-developed animal, coming up from
a plant, — perhaps a link from plant to animal.
In memory, perhaps, of a previous woodland
life, he fills his stomach with pine-knots, and bits
of board, wherever he can find one to chew. It
is his way of taking tobacco. I have been with
a hunter who dissected one of these creatures,
and seen him take from his stomach a mass of
mingled pine-knots, with bits of brick, worn
smooth, as if the digestive fluids had somewhat
corroded them. The fore leg and paw of the
alligator has a pitiful and rather shocking resem-

blance to a black human hand; and the muscular power is so great, that in case of the particular alligator I speak of, even after his head was taken off, when the incision was made into the pectoral muscle for the purpose of skinning, this black hand and arm rose up, and gave the operator quite a formidable push in the chest.

We hope to see some of these creatures out; but none appear. The infrequency of their appearance marks the lateness and backwardness of our spring. There! — a cry of victory is heard from the forward boat; and Mademoiselle Nelly is seen energetically working her elbows: a scuffle ensues, and the captive has a free berth on a boat, without charge for passage-ticket. We shout like people who are getting hungry, as in truth we are. And now Elsie starts in our boat; and all is commotion, till a fine blue bream, spotted with black, is landed. Next a large black trout, with his wide yellow mouth,

comes up unwillingly from the crystal flood. We
pity them; but what are we to do? It is a
question between dinner and dinner. These fish,
out marketing on their own account, darted at
our hook, expecting to catch another fish. We
catch them; and, instead of eating, they are
eaten.

After all, the instinct of hunting and catching
something is as strong in the human breast as in
that of cat or tiger; and we all share the exultation which sends a shout from boat to boat as a
new acquisition is added to our prospective
dinner-store.

And now right in front of us looms up from
the depth of a group of pines and magnolias a
white skeleton of a tree, with gnarled arms,
bleached by years of wind and sun, swathed
with long waving folds of gray moss. On the
very tip-top of this, proudly above all possibility
of capture, a fish-hawk's nest is built. Full

eighty feet in the air, and about the size of
a flour-barrel ; built like an old marauding
baron's stronghold in the middle ages, in inaccessible fastnesses ; lined within and swathed
without with gray moss, — it is a splendid post of
observation. We can see the white head and
shoulders of the bird perched upon her nest ;
and already they perceive us. The pair rise
and clap their wings, and discourse to each
other with loud, shrill cries, perhaps of indigna
tion, that we who have houses to dwell in, and
beef and chickens to eat, should come up and
invade their fishing-grounds.

The fish-hawk — I beg his pardon, the fish-
eagle ; for I can see that he is a bird of no mean
size and proportions — has as good a right to
think that the river and the fish were made for
him as we ; and better too, because the Creator
has endowed him with wonderful eyesight, which
enables him, from the top of a tree eighty feet

high, to search the depths of the river, mark his prey, and dive down with unerring certainty to it. He has his charter in his eyes, his beak, his claws ; and doubtless he has a right to remonstrate, when we, who have neither eyes, beaks, nor claws adapted to the purpose, manage to smuggle away his dinner. Thankful are we that no mighty hunter is aboard, and that the atrocity of shooting a bird on her nest will not be perpetrated here. We are a harmless company, and mean so well by them, that they really might allow us one dinner out of their larder.

We have rowed as far up Julington as is expedient, considering that we have to row down again ; and so we land in the immediate vicinity of our fish-eagle's fortress, greatly to his discontent. Wild, piercing cries come to us now and then from the heights of the eyry ; but we, unmoved, proceed with our dinner-preparations.

Do you want to know the best way in the world of cooking fish ? Then listen.

The fish are taken to the river by one, and simply washed of their superfluous internals, though by no means scaled. A moment prepares them for the fire. Meanwhile a broad hole has been dug in the smooth white sand ; and a fire of dry light wood is merrily crackling therein. The kerosene-stove is set a-going ; the tea-kettle filled, and put on to boil ; when we disperse to examine the palmetto-jungles. One or two parties take to the boats, and skim a little distance up stream, where was a grove of youthful palmetto-trees. The palmetto-shrub is essentially a different variety from the tree. In moist, rich land, the shrub rears a high head, and looks as if it were trying to become a tree ; but it never does it. The leaf, also, is essentially different. The full-grown palm-leaf is three or four yards long, curiously plaited and folded.

In the centre of both palmetto and palm is the bud from whence all future leaves spring, rising like a green spike. This bud is in great request for palmetto-hats ; and all manner of palm-work ; and it was for these buds that our boating-party was going. A venturesome boy, by climbing a neighboring tree and jumping into the palm, can succeed in securing this prize, though at some risk of life and limb. Our party returned with two palm-buds about two yards long, and one or two of the long, graceful leaves.

But now the fire has burned low, and the sand-hole is thoroughly heated. " Bring me," says the presiding cook, " any quantity of those great broad bonnet-leaves." And forth impetuous rush the youth ; and bonnet-leaves cool and dripping are forthcoming, wherewith we double-line the hole in the sand. Then heads and points, compactly folded, go in a line of fish, and are covered down green and comfortable with a double blanket of dripping bonnet-leaves. Then, with a flat board for our shovel, we rake back first the hot sand, and then the coals and brands yet remaining of the fire. Watches are looked at ; and it is agreed by old hands experienced in clam-bakes that half an hour shall be given to complete our dinner.

Meanwhile the steaming tea-kettle calls for coffee, and the French coffee-pot receives its fragrant store ; while the fish-hawk, from his high tower of observation, interjects plaintive notes of remonstrance. I fancy him some hoarse old moralist, gifted with uncomfortable keen-sightedness, forever shrieking down protests on the ways of the thoughtless children of men.

What are we doing to those good fish of his, which he could prepare for the table in much shorter order ? An old hunter who has sometimes explored the ground under the fish-hawk's

6

nest says that bushels of fish-bones may be found there, neatly picked, testifying to the excellent appetite which prevails in those cloud-regions, and to the efficiency of the plan of eating fish *au naturel.*

We wander abroad, and find great blue and white violets and swamp-azaleas along the river's brink; and we take advantage of the not very dense shade of a long-leaved pine to set out the contents of our luncheon-baskets. Ham-sandwiches, hard-boiled eggs, cakes in tempting variety, jellies and fruits, make their appearance in a miscellaneous sort of way. And now comes the great operation of getting out our fish. Without shovel, other than a bit of inflammable pine-board, the thing presents evident difficulties: but it must be done; and done it is.

A platter is improvised of two large palmetto-leaves. The fire is raked off, and the fish emerge

from their baking-place, somewhat the worse as
to external appearance ; but we bear them off to
the feast.   In the trial process we find that the
whole external part of the fish — scales, skin, and
fins — comes off, leaving the meat white and
pure, and deliciously juicy.   A bit well salted and
peppered is forthwith transferred to each plate ;
and all agree that never fish was better and
sweeter.   Then coffee is served round ; and we
feast, and are merry.   When the meal is over, we
arrange our table for the benefit of the fish-
hawks.   The fragments of fish yet remaining,
bits of bread and cake and cheese, are all sys-
tematically arranged for him to take his luncheon
after we are gone.   Mr. Bergh himself could not
ask more exemplary conduct.

For now the westering sun warns us that it is
time to be spreading our sails homeward ; and,
well pleased all, we disperse ourselves into our
respective boats, to fish again as we pass the

lily-pads on the shore.   The sport engages every one on board except myself, who, sitting in the end of the boat, have leisure to observe the wonderful beauty of the sky, the shadows of the forests-belts in the water, and the glorious trees.

One magnolia I saw that deserved to be called an archangel among the sons of the forest.   Full a hundred feet high it stood, with a trunk rising straight, round, and branchless for full fifty feet, and crowned with a glorious head of rich, dark, shining leaves.   When its lily-blossoms awake, what a glory will it become, all alone out there in the silent forest, with only God to see!

No : let us believe, with Milton, that

" Millions of spiritual creatures walk the earth
    Unseen, both when we wake and when we sleep ; "

and the great magnolia-trees may spring and flower for them.

The fishing luck still continues ; and the prospects for a breakfast to-morrow morning are bright. One great fellow, however, makes off with hook, spoon, and all; and we see him floundering among the lily-pads with it in his mouth, vastly dissatisfied with his acquisition. Like many a poor fellow in the world's fishing, he has snapped at a fine bait, and got a sharp hook for his pains.

Now we come back to the yachts, and the fishing is over. The sun is just going down as we raise our white sails and away for the broad shining expanse of the St. John's. In a moment the singers of our party break forth into song and glee ; and catches roll over the water from one yacht to the other as we race along neck and neck.

The evening wind rises fresh and fair, and we sweep down the beautiful coast. Great bars of opal and rose-color lie across the western sky :

the blue waves turn rosy, and ripple and sparkle
with the evening light, as we fly along. On the
distant wharf we see all the stay-at-homes
watching for us as we come to land after the
most successful picnic that heart could conceive.
Each fisherwoman has her fish to exhibit, and
her exploits to recount ; and there is a plentiful
fish-breakfast in each of the houses.

So goes the 29th of February on the St.
John's.

MAGNOLIA.

MANDARIN, FLA., March 6, 1872.

MAGNOLIA is a name suggestive of beauty; and, for once, the name does not belie the fact. The boarding-house there is about the pleasantest winter resort in Florida. We have been passing a day and night there as guest of some friends, and find a company of about seventy people enjoying themselves after the usual fashions of summer watering-places. The house is situated on a

87

little eminence, and commands a fine sweep of view both up and down the river. In the usual fashion of Southern life, it is surrounded with wide verandas, where the guests pass most of their time, — the ladies chatting, and working embroidery ; the gentlemen reading newspapers, and smoking.

The amusements are boating and fishing parties of longer or shorter duration, rides and walks along the shore, or croquet on a fine, shady croquet-ground in a live-oak grove back of the house.

We tried them all. First we went in a rowboat about a couple of miles up a little creek. The shore on either side was ruffled with the green bonnet-leaves, with here and there a golden blossom. The forest-trees, which were large and lofty, were almost entirely of the deciduous kind, which was just bursting into leaf ; and the effect was very curious and

peculiar. One has often remarked what a misty
effect the first buddings of foliage have. Here
there was a mist of many colors, — rose-colored,
pink, crimson, yellow, and vivid green, the hues
of the young leaves, or of the different tags and
keys of the different species of trees. Here and
there a wild plum, sheeted in brilliant white,
varied the tableau. We rowed up to shore, drew
down a branch, and filled the laps of the ladies
with sprays of white flowers. The sun beat
down upon us with the power of August ; and,
had it not been for the fresh breeze that blew up
from the creek, we should have found it very
oppressive. We returned just in time to rest for
dinner. The dining-hall is spacious and cheerful ; and the company are seated at small tables,
forming social groups and parties. The fare was
about the same as would be found in a first-class
boarding-house at the North. The house is
furnished throughout in a very agreeable style ;

and an invalid could nowhere in Florida have more comforts. It is more than full, and constantly obliged to turn away applicants ; and we understand that families are now waiting at Green Cove for places to be vacated here. We are told that it is in contemplation, another season, to put up several cottages, to be rented to families who will board at the hotel. At present there is connected with the establishment one house and a cottage, where some of the guests have their rooms ; and, as the weather is so generally mild, even invalids find no objection to walking to their meals.

The house is a respectable, good-sized, old-fashioned structure ; and, being away from the main building, is preferred by some who feel the need of more entire quiet. Sitting on the front steps in the warm afternoon sunshine, and looking across to the distant, hazy shores, miles away, one could fancy one's self in Italy, — an illusion which the great clumps of aloes, and the tall green yuccas, and the gold-fruited orange-trees, help to carry out. Groups of ladies were seated here and there under trees, reading, working, and chatting. We were called off by the making-up of a croquet-party.

The croquet-ground is under the shade of a fine grove of live-oaks, which, with their sway-ing drapery of white moss, form a graceful shade and shelter. We shared the honor of gaining a victory or two under the banner of a doctor of divinity, accustomed, we believe, to winning laurels on quite other fields in the good city of New York. It has been our general experience, however, that a man good for any thing else is commonly a good croquet-player. We would notify your editor-in-chief, that, if ever he plays a game against Dr. C——, he will find a foeman worthy of his steel.

In the evening the whole company gathered

in the parlors, made cheerful by blazing wood-
fires. There were song-singing and piano-play-
ing, charades and games, to pass the time
withal ; and all bore testimony to the very
sociable and agreeable manner in which life
moved on in their circle.

Magnolia is about three-quarters of a mile
from Green-Cove Springs, where are two or
three large, well-kept boarding-houses. There
is a very pleasant, shady walk through the
woods from one place to the other ; and the mail
comes every day to Green Cove, and is sent for,
from the Magnolia House, in a daily morning
carriage. It is one of the amusements of the
guests to ride over, on these occasions, for a
little morning gossip and shopping, as Magnolia,
being quite sequestered, does not present the
opportunity to chaffer even for a stick of candy.
Of course, fair ones that have been accustomed
to the periodical excitement of a shopping-tour

would sink into atrophy without an opportunity to spend something. What they can buy at Green Cove is a matter of indifference. It is the burning of money in idle purses that injures the nervous system.

There are no orange-groves on this side of the river. The orange-trees about the house are entirely of the wild kind ; and, for merely ornamental purposes, no tree more beautiful could be devised. Its vivid green, the deep gold-color of its clusters of fruit, and the exuberance with which it blossoms, all go to recommend it. Formerly there were extensive orange-groves, with thousands of bearing trees, on this side of the river. The frost of 1835 killed the trees, and they have never been reset. Oranges are not, therefore, either cheap or plenty at Magnolia or Green Cove. Nothing shows more strikingly the want of enterprise that has characterized this country than this. Seedling

oranges planted the very next day after the great
frost would have been in bearing ten years after,
and would, ere now, have yielded barrels and
barrels of fruit ; and the trees would have grown
and taken care of themselves. One would have
thought so very simple and easy a measure
would have been adopted.

At eleven o'clock the next morning we took
steamer for Mandarin, and went skimming along
the shores, watching the white-blossoming plum-
trees amid the green of the forest. We stopped
at Hibernia, a pleasant boarding-house on an
island called Fleming's, after a rich Col. Fleming who formerly had a handsome plantation
there. There is a fine, attractive-looking country-house, embowered in trees and with shaded
verandas, where about forty boarders are yearly
accommodated. We have heard this resort very
highly praised as a quiet spot, where the accommodations are homelike and comfortable. It is

kept by the widow of the former proprietor ; and we are told that guests who once go there return year after year. There is something certainly very peaceful and attractive about its surroundings.

But now our boat is once more drawing up to the wharf at Mandarin ; and we must defer much that we have to say till next week. Phœbus, we are happy to say to our girl correspondents, is bright and happy, and in excellent voice. All day long, at intervals, we can hear him from the back veranda, shouting, " What cheer ! what cheer !" or sometimes abbreviating it as " Cheer, cheer, cheer ! "

Since we have been writing, one of those characteristic changes have come up to which this latitude is subject. The sun was shining, the river blue, the windows open, and the family reading, writing, and working on the veranda, when suddenly comes a frown of Nature, — a

black scowl in the horizon.   Up flies the wind;
the waves are all white-caps ; the blinds bang ;
the windows rattle; every one runs to shut every
thing ; and for a few moments it blows as if it
would take house and all away.   Down drop
oranges in a golden shower ; here, there, and
everywhere the lightning flashes ; thunder
cracks and rattles and rolls ; and the big torrents
of rain come pouring down : but, in the back-
porch, Phœbus between each clap persists in
shouting, " What cheer ! what cheer ! "   Like a
woman in a passion, Nature ends all this with a
burst of tears ; and it is raining now, tenderly
and plaintively as if bemoaning itself.

Well, we wouldn't have missed the sight if we
had been asked ; and we have picked up a
bushel of oranges that otherwise somebody must
have climbed the trees for.

Meanwhile the mail is closing.   Good-by !

YELLOW JESSAMINES.

HEY talk about Florida being the land of flowers: I'm sure *I* don't see where the flowers are."

The speaker was a trim young lady, with pretty, high-heeled boots, attired in all those charming mysteries behind and before, and up and down, that make the daughter of Eve look like some bright, strange, tropical bird. She had come to see Florida ; that is, to take board at the St. James. She had provided herself with half a dozen different palmetto-hats, an orange-wood cane tipped with an alligator's tooth, together with an assortment of cranes' wings and pink curlews' feathers, and talked of Florida with the assured air of a connoisseur. She had been on the boat up to Enterprise ; she had crossed at Tekoi over to St. Augustine, and come back to the St. James ; and was now prepared to speak as one having authority : and she was sure she did not see why it was called a land of flowers. *She* hadn't seen any.

"But, my dear creature, have you ever been where they grow? Have you walked in the woods?"

"Walked in the woods? Gracious me! Of course not! Who could walk in sand half up to one's ankles? I tried once ; and the sand got into my boots, and soiled my stockings : besides, I'm afraid of snakes."

"Then, my dear, you will never be a judge on the question whether Florida is or is not a land of flowers. Whoever would judge on that question must make up her mind to good long tramps in the woods; must wear stout boots, with India-rubbers, or, better still, high India-rubber boots. So equipped, and with eyes open to see what is to be seen, you will be prepared to explore those wild glades and mysterious shadows where Nature's beauties, marvels, and mysteries are wrought. The Venus of these woods is only unveiled in their deepest solitudes."

For ourselves, we claim to have experience in this matter of flowers; having always observed them in all lands. We were impressed more by the *flowers* of Italy than by any thing else there; yes, more than by the picture-galleries, the statues, the old ruins. The sight of the green lawns of the Pamfili Doria, all bubbling up in little rainbow-tinted anemones ; the cool dells where we picked great blue-and-white violets ; the damp, mossy shadows in the Quirinal gardens, where cyclamen grow in crimson clouds amid a crush of precious old marbles and antiques ; the lovely flowers, unnamed of botany, but which we should call a sort of glorified blue-and-white daisies, that we gathered in the shadowy dells near Castle Gandolpho, — these have a freshness in our memory that will last when the memory of all the "stun images" of the Vatican has passed away.

In our mind's eye we have compared Florida with Italy often, and asked if it can equal it. The flowers here are not the same, it is true. The blue violets are not fragrant. We do not find the many-colored anemones, nor the cyclamen. Both can be planted out here, and will grow readily ; but they are not *wild* flowers, not indigenous.

"Well, then, are there others to compen-
sate?" We should say so.

The yellow jessamine itself, in its wild grace,
with its violet-scented breath, its profuse abundance, is more than a substitute for the anemones of Italy.

If you will venture to walk a little way in the
sand beyond our back-gate, we will show you a
flower-show this morning such as Chiswick or
the Crystal Palace cannot equal.

About a quarter of a mile we walk: and then
we turn in to what is called here an oak-hammock; which is, being interpreted, a grove of
live-oak-trees, with an underbrush of cedar,
holly, and various flowering-shrubs. An effort
has been made to clear up this hammock. The
larger trees have some of them been cut down,
but not removed. The work of clearing was
abandoned; and, the place being left to Nature,
she proceeded to improve and beautify it after a

fashion of her own. The yellow jessamine,
which before grew under the shadow of the
trees, now, exultant in the sunshine which was
let in upon it, has made a triumphant and
abounding growth, such as we never saw anywhere else. It is the very Ariel of flowers, —
the tricksy sprite, full of life and grace and
sweetness; and it seems to take a capricious
pleasure in rambling everywhere, and masquer-
ading in the foliage of every kind of tree. Now
its yellow bells twinkle down like stars from the
prickly foliage of the holly, where it has
taken full possession, turning the solemn old
evergreen into a blossoming garland. Now,
sure enough, looking up full sixty feet into yonder water-oak, we see it peeping down at us in
long festoons, mingling with the swaying, crapy
streamers of the gray moss. Yonder a little
live-oak-tree has been so completely possessed
and beflowered, that it shows a head of blossoms

as round as an apple-tree in May. You look below, and jessamine is trailing all over the ground, weaving and matting, with its golden buds and open bells peeping up at you from the huckleberry-bushes and sedge-grass.

Here is a tree overthrown, and raising its gaunt, knotted branches in air, veiled with soft mossy drapery. The jessamine springs upon it for a trellis : it weaves over and under and around ; it throws off long sprays and streamers with two golden buds at the axil of every green leaf, and fluttering out against the blue of the sky. Its multiform sprays twist and knot and tie themselves in wonderful intricacies ; and still where every green leaf starts is a yellow flower-bud. The beauty of these buds is peculiar. They have little sculptured grooves ; and the whole looks as if it might have been carved of fairy chrysolite for a lady's ear-drop. Our little brown chambermaid wears them dangling in her ears ; and a very pretty picture she makes with them. Coal-black Frank looks admiringly after her as she trips by with them shaking and twinkling to his confusion, as he forgets for a moment to saw wood, and looks longingly after her. No use, Frank. "Trust her not: she is fooling thee." Her smiles are all for lighter-colored beaux. But still she wears yellow jessamine in her crapy hair, and orders Frank to bring her wreaths and sprays of it whenever she wants it ; and Frank obeys. That's female sovereignty, the world over!

In this same hammock are certain tall, graceful shrubs, belonging, as we fancy, to the high-huckleberry tribe, but which the Floridians call sparkleberry. It is the most beautiful white ornamental shrub we have ever seen. Imagine a shrub with vivid green foliage, hanging profusely with wreaths of lilies-of-the-valley, and you have as near as possible an idea of the sparkleberry. It is only in bud now, being a little later than the jessamine, and coming into its glory when the jessamine is passing away.

The regular employment now of every afternoon is to go out in the mule-cart with old Fly into the woods, flower-hunting.

It is as lovely an afternoon-work as heart could wish; the sky is so blue, the air so balmy, and at every step there is something new to admire. The coming-out of the first leaves and tags and blossom-keys of the deciduous trees has a vividness and brilliancy peculiar to these regions. The oak-hammock we have been describing as the haunt of yellow jessamine is as picturesque and beautiful a tree-study as an artist could desire. There are tall, dark cedars, in which the gray films of the long moss have a peculiarly light and airy appearance. There is the majestic dome of the long-leaved Southern pine, rising high over all the other trees, as in

Italy the stone-pine. Its leaves are from twelve
to eighteen inches long; and the swaying of
such pines makes a *susurrus* worth listening
to. The water-oak is throwing out its bright
young leaves of a gold-tinted green; and the
live-oak, whose leaves are falling now, is bursting into little velvety tags, premonitory of new
foliage. Four species of oaks we notice. The
live-oak, the water-oak, and a species of scrub-
tree which they call the olive-leaved oak, are
all evergreens, and have narrow, smooth leaves.
Then there are what are familiarly called black-
jacks, — a deciduous oak, which bears a large,
sharply-cut, indented leaf, of a character resembling our Northern ones. Besides these, the
prickly-ash, with its curiously knobbed and
pointed branches, and its graceful, featnery
leaves, forms a feature in the scene. Under-
neath, great clumps of prickly-pear are throwing
out their queer buds, to be, in turn, followed by
bright yellow blossoms.

To an uninstructed eye, the pine-woods in which we ride look like a flat, monotonous scene. The pines rise seventy, eighty, and a hundred feet in the air, so that their tops are far above, and cast no shade. This is a consideration of value, however, for a winter's ride; for one enjoys the calm sunshine. Even in days when high winds are prevailing along the river-front, the depth of these pine-woods is calm, sunny, and still; and one can always have a pleasant walk there. When the hotter months come on, the live-oaks and water-oaks have thick, new foliage, and the black-jacks and hickory and sweet-gum trees throw out their shade to shelter the traveller. Every mile or two, our path is traversed by a brook on its way to the St. John's. The natives here call a brook a "branch;" and a branch is no small circumstance, since all the finest trees and shrubbery grow upon its banks. You can look through the high, open pillars of the pine-trees, and watch the course of a branch half a mile from you by the gorgeous vegetation of the trees which line its shores.

We jog along in our mule-cart, admiring every thing as we go. We are constantly exclaiming at something, and tempted to get out to gather flowers. Here and there through the long wire-grass come perfect gushes of blue and white violets. The blue violets are large, and, of necessity, are obliged to put forth very long stems to get above the coarse, matted grass. The white are very fragrant, and perfectly whiten the ground in some moist places. There is a large, fragrant kind, very scarce and rare, but of which we have secured several roots. We are going this afternoon to the "second branch" after azaleas. We stop at a little distance, when its wall of glossy verdure rises up before us. There is no accomplishment of a mule in which Fly is better versed than stopping and standing still. We fancy that we hear him, in his inner consciousness, making a merit of it, as we all do of our pet virtues. He is none of your frisky fellows, always wanting to be going, and endangering everybody that wants to get in or out with prances and curvets, — not he! He is a beast that may be trusted to stand for any length of time without an attempt at motion. Catch *him* running away! So we leave Fly, and determine to explore the branch.

The short palmettoes here are grown to the height of fifteen feet. Their roots look like great scaly serpents, which, after knotting and convoluting a while, suddenly raise their crests high in air, and burst forth into a graceful crest of waving green fans. These waving clumps of fan-like leaves are the first and peculiar feature of the foliage. Along the shore here, clumps of pale pink azaleas grow high up, and fill the

air with sweetness. It is for azaleas we are
come ; and so we tread our way cautiously, —
cautiously, because we have heard tales of the
moccasin-snake — fearful gnome ! — said to infest
damp places, and banks of rivers. In all our
Floridian rambles, we never yet have got sight
of this creature ; though we have explored all
the moist places, and sedgy, swampy dells,
where azaleas and blue iris and white lilies
grow. But the tradition that such things are
inspires a wholesome care never to set a foot
down without looking exactly where it goes.
"The branch," we find, is lighted up in many
places by the white, showy blossoms of the dogwood, of which, also, we gather great store. We
pile in flowers — azalea and dogwood — till our
wagon is full, and then proceed with a trowel to
take up many nameless beauties.

There is one which grows on a high, slender
stalk, resembling in its form a primrose, that has

the purest and intensest yellow that we ever saw in a flower. There is a purple variety of the same species, that grows in the same neighborhoods. We have made a bed of these woodland beauties at the roots of our great oak, so that they may finish their growth, and seed, if possible, under our own eye.

By the by, we take this occasion to tell the lady who writes to beg of us to send her some seeds or roots of Florida plants or flowers, that we have put her letter on file, and perhaps, some day, may find something to send her. Any one who loves flowers touches a kindred spot in our heart. The difficulty with all these flowers and roots sent North is, that they need the heat of this climate to bring them to perfection. Still there is no saying what a real plant-lover may do in coaxing along exotics. The "run" we have been exploring has, we are told, in the season of them, beautiful blue wisteria climbing from branch to branch. It does not come till after the yellow jessamine is gone. The coral-honeysuckle and a species of trumpet-creeper also grow here, and, in a little time, will be in full flower. One of our party called us into the run, and bade us admire a beautiful shrub, some fifteen feet high, whose curious, sharply-cut, deep-green leaves were shining with that glossy polish which gives such brilliance. Its leaves were of waxen thickness, its habit of growth peculiarly graceful ; and our colored handmaiden, who knows the habits of every plant in our vicinity, tells us that it bears a white, sweet blossom, some weeks later. We mentally resolve to appropriate this fair Daphne of the woods on the first opportunity when hands can be spared to take it up and transport it.

But now the sun falls west, and we plod homeward. If you want to see a new and peculiar beauty, watch a golden sunset through

a grove draperied with gray moss. The swaying, filmy bands turn golden and rose-colored ;
and the long, swaying avenues are like a scene
in fairyland. We come home, and disembark
our treasures. Our house looks like a perfect
flower-show. Every available vase and jar is
full, — dogwood, azaleas, blue iris, wreaths of
yellow jessamine, blue and white violets, and
the golden unknown, which we christen prim-
roses. The daily sorting of the vases is no
small charge : but there is a hand to that department which never neglects ; and so we breathe
their air and refresh our eyes with their beauty
daily.

Your cold Northern snow-storms hold back
our spring. The orange-buds appear, but hang
back. They are three weeks later than usual.
Our letters tell us frightful stories of thermome-
ters no end of the way below zero. When you
have a snow-storm, we have a cold rain : so you

8

must keep bright lookout on your ways up there, or we shall get no orange-blossoms.

We have received several letters containing questions about Florida. It is our intention to devote our next paper to answering these. We are perfectly ready to answer any number of inquiries, so long as we can lump them all together, and answer them through "The Christian Union."

One class of letters, however, we cannot too thankfully remember. Those who have read our papers with so much of sympathy as to send in contributions to our church here have done us great good. We have now a sum contributed with which we hope soon to replace our loss. And now, as the mail is closing, we must close.

P. S. — We wish you could see a gigantic bouquet that Mr. S—— has just brought in from the hummock. A little shrub-oak, about five feet high, whose spreading top is all a golden mass of bloom with yellow jessamine, he has cut down, and borne home in triumph.

What an adornment would this be for one of the gigantic Japanese vases that figure in New-York drawing-rooms! What would such a bouquet sell for?

"FLORIDA FOR INVALIDS."

WE find an aggrieved feeling in the minds of the Floridian public in view of a letter in " The Independent," by Dr. ——, headed as above ; and we have been urgently requested to say something on the other view of the question.

Little did we suppose when we met our good friend at Magnolia, apparently in the height of spirits, the life of the establishment, and head promoter of all sorts of hilarity, that, under all this delightful cheerfulness, he was contending with such dreary experiences as his article in " The Independent " would lead one to suppose. Really, any one who should know the doctor only from that article might mistake him for a wretched hypochondriac ; whereas we saw him, and heard of him by universal repute at Magnolia, as one of the cheeriest and sunniest of the inmates, taking every thing by the smoothest handle, and not only looking on the bright side himself, but making everybody else do the same. Imagine, therefore, our utter astonishment at finding our buoyant doctor summing up his Florida experience in such paragraphs as these : —

" From what I have observed, I should think Florida was nine-tenths water, and the other tenth swamp. Many are deceived by the milder climate here ; and down they come — to die. The mildness, too, is exaggerated. Yesterday morning, the thermometer was at thirty-six degrees. Outside, our winter overcoats were necessary; and great wood-fires roared within. Now and then the thermometer reaches eighty degrees at mid-day; but, that very night, you may have frost.

"Another fact of Florida is malaria. How could it be otherwise? Souse Manhattan Island two feet deep in fresh water, and wouldn't the price of quinine rise?

"I have no objection to the term 'sunny South;' it is a pretty alliteration: but I object to its application to Georgia and Florida in February. I wish you could have seen me last Friday night. We were riding two hundred and sixty miles through a swamp, — Okefinokee of the geographies. I was clad in full winter suit, with heavy Russian overcoat."

But a careful comparison of the incidents in his letter solves the mystery. The letter was written in an early date in the doctor's Floridian experience, and before he had had an opportunity of experiencing the benefit which he subsequently reaped from it.

We perceive by the reference to last Friday night, and the ride through Okefinokee Swamp, that the doctor was then fresh from the North, and undergoing that process of disenchantment which many Northern travellers experience, particularly those who come by railroad. The most ardent friends of Florida must admit that this railroad is by no means a prepossessing approach to the land of promise ; and the midnight cold upon it is something likely to be had in remembrance. When we crossed it, however, we had a stove, which was a small imitation of Nebuchadnezzar's furnace, to keep us in heart. Otherwise there is a great deal of truth in our friend's allegations. As we have elsewhere remarked, every place, like a bit of tapestry, has its right side and its wrong side ; and both are true and real, — the wrong side with its tags and rags, and seams and knots, and thrums of worsted, and the right side with its pretty picture.

It is true, as the doctor says, that some invalids do come here, expose themselves imprudently, and die. People do die in Florida, if they use the means quite as successfully as in New York. It is true that sometimes the thermometer stands at seventy at noon, and that the nights are much cooler; it is true we have sometimes severe frosts in Florida ; it is true we have malaria ; it is true that there are swamps in Florida ; and it is quite apt to be true, that, if a man rides a hundred miles through a swamp at night, he will feel pretty chilly.

All these are undeniable truths. We never pretended that Florida was the kingdom of heaven, or the land where they shall no more say, "I am sick." It is quite the reverse. People this very winter have in our neighborhood had severe attacks of pneumonia ; and undoubtedly many have come to Florida seeking health, and have not found it.

Yet, on the other hand, there are now living in Florida many old established citizens and land-owners who came here ten, twenty, and thirty years ago, given over in consumption, who have here for years enjoyed a happy and vigorous life in spite of Okefinokee Swamp and the malaria.

Undoubtedly the country would be much better to live in if there were no swamps and no malaria ; and so, also, New England would be better to live in if there were not six months winter and three more months of cold weather there. As to malaria, it is not necessary to souse Manhattan Island under water to get that in and around New York. The new lands in

New York will give you chills and fever quite as well as Florida. You can find malarial fevers almost anywhere in the towns between New York and New Haven ; and it is notorious that many estates in the vicinity of New York and Philadelphia sell cheap on that very account, because they are almost as malarious as some Italian villas.

Florida is not quite so bad as that yet, although it has its share of that malaria which attends the development of land in a new country. But the malarial fevers here are of a mild type, and easily managed ; and they are generally confined to the fall months. The situation of Florida, surrounded by the sea, and the free sweep of winds across it, temper the air, and blow away malarious gases.

In regard to consumptives and all other invalids, the influence of a Floridian climate depends very much on the nature of the case and the constitution of the individual.

If persons suffer constitutionally from cold ; if they are bright and well only in hot weather ; if the winter chills and benumbs them, till, in the spring, they are in the condition of a frost-bitten hot-house plant, — alive, to be sure, but with every leaf gone, — then these persons may be quite sure that they will be the better for a winter in Florida, and better still if they can take up their abode there.

But if, on the contrary, persons are debilitated and wretched during hot weather, and if cool weather braces them, and gives them vigor and life, then such evidently have no call to Florida, and should be booked for Minnesota, or some other dry, cold climate. There are consumptives belonging to both these classes of constitution ; and the coming of one of the wrong kind to Florida is of no use to himself, and is sure to bring discredit on the country. A little good common sense and reflection will settle that matter.

Again : there is a form of what passes for consumption, which is, after all, some modification of liver-complaint; and, so far as we have heard or observed, Florida is no place for these cases. The diseases here are of the bilious type ; and those who have liver-complaint are apt to grow worse rather than better.   But there are classes of persons on whom the climate of Florida acts like a charm.

There are certain nervously-organized dyspeptics who require a great deal of open, out-door life.   They are in comfortable health during those months when they can spend half their time in the open air.   They have no particular disease ; but they have no great reserved strength, and cannot battle with severe weather They cannot go out in snow or wind, or on chilly, stormy days, without risking more harm than they get good.   Such, in our Northern climate, are kept close prisoners for six months.

From December to May, they are shut in to furnace-heated houses or air-tight stoves. The winter is one long struggle to keep themselves up. For want of the out-door exercise which sustains them in summer, appetite and sleep both fail them. They have restless nights and bad digestion, and look anxiously to the end of winter as the only relief. For such how slowly it drags! They watch the almanac. The sun crosses the line; the days grow a minute longer: spring will come by and by. But by what cruel irony was the month of March ever called spring? — March, which piles snow-storms and wind-storms on backs almost broken by endurance. The long agony of March and April is the breaking-point with many a delicate person who has borne pretty well the regular winter.

Said one who did much work, "I bear it pretty well through December. I don't so much

mind January. February tires me a little; but I
face it bravely. But by March I begin to say,
'Well, if this don't stop pretty soon, *I* shall: I
can't get much farther.'" But our heaviest
snow-storms and most savage cold are often
reserved for March; and to many an invalid it
has given the final thrust: it is the last straw
that breaks the camel's back. But after March,
in New England, comes April, utterly untrust-
worthy, and with no assured out-door life for a
delicate person. As to the month of May, the
poet Cowper has a lively poem ridiculing the
poets who have made the charms of May the subject of their songs. Mother Nature is represented as thus addressing them : —

> "'Since you have thus combined,' she said,
>   'My favorite nymph to slight,
>   Adorning May, that peevish maid,
>   With June's undoubted right,

> The minx, cursed for your folly's sake,
>   Shall prove herself a shrew ;
> Shall make your scribbling fingers ache,
>   And bite your noses blue.' "

Which she generally does.

So it is not really till June that delicately-constituted persons, or persons of impaired vigor, really feel themselves out of prison. They have then about five months at most in which they can live an open-air life, before the prison-doors close on them again.

Now, the persons who would be most benefited by coming to Florida are not the desperately diseased, the confirmed consumptives, but those of such impaired physical vigor that they are in danger of becoming so. An ounce of prevention here is worth many pounds of cure. It is too often the case that the care and expense that might have prevented disease from settling are spent in vain after it has once fastened. Sad it is indeed to see the wan and wasted faces, and hear the hollow death-cough, of those who have been brought here too late. Yet, in hundreds of instances, yes, in thousands, where one more severe Northern winter would have fastened disease on the vitals, a winter in a Southern climate has broken the spell. The climate of Florida is also of peculiar advantage in all diseases attended by nervous excitability. The air is peculiarly soothing and tranquillizing: it is the veritable lotos-eater's paradise, full of quiet and repose. We have known cases where the sleeplessness of years has given way, under this balmy influence, to the most childlike habit of slumber.

For debility, and the complaints that spring from debility, Florida is not so good a refuge, perhaps, as some more northern point, like Aiken. The air here is soothing, but not particularly bracing. It builds up and strengthens, not by any tonic effect in itself so much as by the opportunity for constant open-air life and exercise which it affords.

For children, the climate cannot be too much praised. In our little neighborhood are seven about as lively youngsters as could often be met with ; and the winter has been one long out-door play-spell. There has not been a cough, nor a cold, nor an ailment of any kind, and scarce an anxiety. All day long we hear their running and racing, — down to the boat-wharves ; in the boats, which they manage as dexterously as little Sandwich - Islanders ; fishing ; catching crabs, or off after flowers in the woods, with no trouble of hail, sleet, or wet feet. Truly it is a child's Eden ; and they grow and thrive accordingly.

Now as to malaria. That is a word requiring consideration to those who expect to make Florida a permanent home, but having no terrors

9

for those who come to spend winters merely
There is no malaria in winter; and Dr. C——
may be consoled in reflecting that frost always
destroys it: so that, when the thermometer is, as
he says, at thirty-two degrees, there is no danger,
even though one be in the same State with forty
swamps. In fact, for ourselves, we prefer a cool
winter such as this has been. An October-like
winter, when it is warm in the middle of the
day, and one can enjoy a bright fire on the
hearth morning and night, is the most favorable
to out-door exercise and to health.

But merely to come to Florida, and idle away
time at the St. James or the St. Augustine
Hotel, taking no regular exercise, and having no
employment for mind or body, is no way to improve by being here. It is because the climate
gives opportunity of open-air exercise that it is
so favorable; but, if one neglects all these opportunities, he may gain very little.

It cannot be too often impressed on strangers coming here, that what cold there is will be more keenly ·felt than in a Northern climate. Persons should vary their clothing carefully to the varying temperature, and be quite as careful to go warmly clad as in colder States. In our furnace-heated houses at the North we generally wear thick woollen dresses and under-flannels, and keep up a temperature of from seventy to eighty degrees. In the South we move in a much lower temperature, and have only the open fire upon the hearth. It is therefore important to go warmly clad, and particularly to keep on flannels until the warm weather of April becomes a settled thing.

In regard to the healthfulness of Florida, some things are to be borne in mind. In a State that has the reputation of being an inva lid's asylum, many desperate cases necessarily take refuge, and, of course, many die. Yet, notwithstanding the loss from these causes, the census of 1860 showed that the number of deaths from pulmonary complaints is less to the population than in any State of the Union. In Massachusetts, the rate is one in two hundred and fifty-four; in California, one in seven hundred and twenty-seven; in Florida, one in fourteen hundred and forty-seven. Surgeon-Gen. Lawson of the United-States army, in his report, asserts that "the ratio of deaths to the number of cases of remittent fevers has been much less among the troops serving in Florida than in other portions of the United States. In the middle division, the proportion is one death to thirty-six cases of fever; in the northern, one to fifty-two; in Texas, one to seventy-eight; in California, one in a hundred and twenty-two; while in Florida it is one in two hundred and eighty-seven."

Such statistics as these are more reliable than

the limited observation of any one individual. In regard to sudden changes of climate, Florida is certainly not in all parts ideally perfect. There are, at times, great and sudden changes there, but not by any means as much so as in most other States of the Union.

Sudden changes from heat to cold are the besetting sin of this fallen world. It is the staple subject for grumbling among the invalids who visit Italy ; and, in fact, it is probably one of the consequences of Adam's fall, which we are not to be rid of till we get to the land of pure delight. It may, however, comfort the hearts of visitors to Florida to know, that, if the climate here is not in this respect just what they would have it, it is about the best there is going.

All this will be made quite clear to any one who will study the tables of observations on temperature contained in " The Guide to Florida," where they can see an accurate account of the range of the thermometer for five successive years as compared with that in other States.

One thing cannot be too often reiterated to people who come to Florida ; and that is, that they must not expect at once to leave behind them all sickness, sorrow, pain, inconvenience of any kind, and to enter at once on the rest of paradise.

The happiness, after all, will have to be comparative ; and the inconveniences are to be borne by reflecting how much greater inconveniences are avoided. For instance, when we have a three-days' damp, drizzling rain-storm down here, we must reflect, that, at the North, it is a driving snow-storm. When it is brisk, cold weather here, it is an intolerable freeze there. The shadow and reflection of all important changes at the North travel down to us in time. The exceptionally cold winter at the North has put our season here back a month behind its usual spring-time. The storms travel down-ward, coming to us, generally, a little later, and in a modified form.

We cannot better illustrate this than by two experiences this year. Easter morning we were waked by bird-singing ; and it was a most heavenly morning. We walked out in the calm, dewy freshness, to gather flowers to dress our house, — the only church we have now in which to hold services. In the low swamp-land 'near our home is a perfect field of blue iris, whose bending leaves were all beaded with dew ; and we walked in among them, admiring the won-derful vividness of their coloring, and gathering the choicest to fill a large vase. Then we cut verbenas, white, scarlet, and crimson, rose-gera-niums and myrtle, callas and roses ; while already on our tables were vases of yellow jes-samine, gathered the night before. The blue St. John's lay in misty bands of light and shade in the distance; and the mocking-birds and red-birds were singing a loud *Te Deum*.

Now for the North. A friend in Hartford writes, "I was awaked by the patter of snow and sleet on the window-pane. Not a creature could go out to church, the storm was so severe: even the Irish were obliged to keep housed. With all we could do with a furnace and morning-glory stove, we could not get the temperature of our house above fifty-five degrees."

In the latter part of the day, we at Mandarin had some rough, chilling winds, which were the remains of the Northern Easter storm; but we were wise enough to rejoice in the good we had, instead of fretting at the shadow of evil.

SWAMPS AND ORANGE-TREES.

AFTER a cold, damp, rainy week, we have suddenly had dropped upon us a balmy, warm, summer day, — thermometer at eighty ; and every thing out of doors growing so fast, that you may see and hear it grow.

The swampy belt of land in front of the house is now bursting forth in clouds of blue iris of every shade, from the palest and faintest

137

to the most vivid *lapis-lazuli* tint.   The wild-
rose-bushes there are covered with buds ; and
the cypress-trees are lovely with their vivid little feathers of verdure.   This swamp is one of
those crooks in our lot which occasions a never-
ceasing conflict of spirit.   It is a glorious, bewil-
dering impropriety.   The trees and shrubs in it
grow as if they were possessed ; and there is
scarcely a month in the 'year that it does not
flame forth in some new blossom.   It is a per-
petual flower-garden, where creepers run and
tangle ; where Nature has raptures and frenzies
of growth, and conducts herself like a crazy,
drunken, but beautiful *bacchante.*   But what to
do with it is not clear.   The river rises and
falls in it ; and under all that tangle of foliage
lies a foul sink of the blackest mud.   The
black, unsavory moccasin-snakes are said and
believed to have their lair in those jungles,
where foot of man cares not to tread.   Gi-

gantic bulrushes grow up ; clumps of high
water-grasses, willows, elms, maples, cypresses,
Magnolia glauca (sweet-bay), make brave show
of foliage. Below, the blue pickerel-weed, the
St. John's lily, the blue iris, wild-roses, blossoming tufts of elder, together with strange flowers
of names unspoken, make a goodly fellowship.
The birds herd there in droves ; red-birds glance
like gems through the boughs ; cat-birds and
sparrows and jays babble and jargon there in
the green labyrinths made by the tangling vines.
We muse over it, meanwhile enjoying the visible
coming-on of spring in its foliage. The maples
have great red leaves, curling with their own
rapid growth ; the elms feather out into graceful
plumes ; and the cypress, as we said before,
most brilliant of all spring greens, puts forth its
fairy foliage. Verily it is the most gorgeous of
improprieties, this swamp ; and we will let it
alone this year also, and see what will come of

it.   There are suggestions of ditching and draining, and what not, that shall convert the wild *bacchante* into a steady, orderly member of society.   We shall see.

Spring is a glory anywhere ; but, as you approach the tropics, there is a vivid brilliancy, a burning tone, to the coloring, that is peculiar. We are struck with the beauty of the cat-briers. We believe they belong to the smilax family ; and the kinds that prevail here are evergreen, and have quaintly-marked leaves.   Within a day or two, these glossy, black-green vines have thrown out trembling red sprays shining with newness, with long tendrils waving in the air. The vigor of a red young shoot that seems to spring out in an hour has something delightful in it.

Yellow jessamine, alas ! is fading.   The ground is strewn with pale-yellow trumpets, as if the elves had had a concert and thrown down their instruments, and fled. Now the vines throw out young shoots half a yard long, and infinite in number; and jessamine goes on to possess and clothe new regions, which next February shall be yellow with flowers.

Farewell for this year, sweet Medea of the woods, with thy golden fleece of blossoms! Why couldst thou not stay with us through the year? Emerson says quaintly, "Seventy salads measure the life of a man." The things, whether of flower or fruit, that we can have but once a year, mark off our lives. · A lover might thus tell the age of his lady-love : "Seventeen times had the jessamine blossomed since she came into the world." The time of the bloom of the jessamine is about two months. In the middle of January, when we came down, it was barely budded : the 25th of March, and it is past.

But, not to give all our time to flowers, we

must now fulfil our promise to answer letters, and give practical information.

A gentleman propounds to us the following inquiry: "Apart from the danger from frosts, what is the prospect of certainty in the orange-crop? Is it a steady one?"

We have made diligent inquiry from old, experienced cultivators, and from those who have collected the traditions of orange-growing; and the result seems to be, that, apart from the danger of frost, the orange-crop is the most steady and certàin of any known fruit.

In regard to our own grove, consisting of a hundred and fifteen trees on an acre and a half of ground, we find that there has been an average crop matured of sixty thousand a year for each of the five years we have had it. Two years the crop was lost through sudden frost coming after it was fully perfected; but these two years are the only ones since 1835 when a crop has been lost or damaged through frost.

Our friend inquires with regard to the orange-insect. This was an epidemic which prevailed some fifteen or twenty years ago, destroying the orange-trees as the canker-worms did the apple-trees. It was a variety of the scale-bug; but nothing has been seen of it in an epidemic form for many years, and growers now have no apprehensions from this source.

The wonderful vital and productive power of the orange-tree would not be marvelled at could one examine its roots. The ground all through our grove is a dense mat or sponge of fine yellow roots, which appear like a network on the least displacing of the sand. Every ramification has its feeder, and sucks up food for the tree with avidity. The consequence is, that people who have an orange-grove must be contented with that, and not try to raise flowers ; but, nev-

ertheless, we do try, because we can't help it
But every fertilizer that we put upon our roses
and flower-beds is immediately rushed after by
these hungry yellow orange-roots. At the root
of our great live-oak we wanted a little pet colony
of flowers, and had muck and manure placed
there to prepare for them. In digging there
lately, we found every particle of muck and
manure netted round with the fine, embracing
fibres from the orange-tree ten feet off. The
consequence is, that our roses grow slowly, and
our flower-garden is not a success.

Oleanders, cape-jessamines, pomegranates, and
crape-myrtles manage, however, to stand their
ground. Any strong, woody-fibred plant does
better than more delicate flowers ; as people who
will insist upon their rights, and fight for them,
do best in the great scramble of life.

But what a bouquet of sweets is an orange-
tree ! Merely as a flowering-tree it is worth

having, if for nothing else. We call the time of their budding the week of pearls. How beauti‧ful, how almost miraculous, the leaping-forth of these pearls to gem the green leaves ! The fragrance has a stimulating effect on our nerves, — a sort of dreamy intoxication. The air, now, is full of it. Under the trees the white shell-petals drift, bearing perfume.

But, not to lose our way in poetic raptures, we return to statistics drawn from a recent conversation with our practical neighbor. He has three trees in his grounds, which this year have each borne five thousand oranges. He says that he has never failed of a steady crop from any cause, except in the first of the two years named ; and, in that case, it is to be remembered the fruit was perfected, and only lost by not being gathered.

He stated that he had had reports from two men whom he named, who had each gathered

ten thousand from a single tree. He appeared
to think it a credible story, though a very
remarkable yield.

The orange can be got from seed. Our
neighbor's trees, the largest and finest in
Mandarin, are seedlings. Like ours, they
were frozen down in 1835, and subsequently
almost destroyed by the orange-insect; but
now they are stately, majestic trees of wonderful beauty. The orange follows the quality,
of the seed, and needs no budding ; and in our
region this mode of getting the trees is univer-
sally preferred. Fruit may be expected from the
seed in six years, when high cultivation is practised. A cultivator in our neighborhood saw a
dozen trees, with an average of three hundred
oranges on each, at seven years from the seed.
Young seedling plants of three years' growth
can be bought in the nurseries on the St. John's
River.

Our young folks have been thrown into a state of great excitement this afternoon by the introduction among them of two live alligators. Our friend Mr. P—— went for them to the lair of the old alligator, which he describes as a hole in the bank, where the eggs are laid. Hundreds of little alligators were crawling in and out, the parents letting them shift for themselves. They feed upon small fish. Our young *protégé* snapped in a very suggestive manner at a stick offered to him, and gave an energetic squeak. We pointed out to the children, that, if it were their finger or toe that was in the stick's place, the consequences might be serious. After all, we have small sympathy with capturing these poor monsters. We shall have some nice tales to tell of them anon. Meanwhile our paper must end here.

LETTER-WRITING.

OUR Palmetto correspondence increases daily. Our mail comes only twice a week ; and, as the result of the two last mails, we find fifteen letters, propounding various inquiries about Florida. Now, it would be a most delightful thing to be on sociable terms with all the world ; and we would be glad to reply to each one of these letters. Many of them are sprightly and amusing : all are writ-

148

ten in good faith, containing most natural and
rational inquiries. But, let any one attempt the
task of writing fifteen letters on one subject,
and he will soon find that it is rather more than
can be done by one who expects to do any thing
else.

Some of the inquiries, however, we may as
well dispose of in the beginning of this letter.

And first as to the little boy who has lost his
cat, and wishes to know if we cannot spare
Peter to take her place. Alas! we have a tale
of sadness to unfold. When we began our
" Palmetto-Leaves," we were the embarrassed
possessor of four thrifty cats: now every one
of them has passed to the land of shades, and
we are absolutely *catless*. Peter, we regret to
say, was killed in consequence of being mis-
taken for a rabbit, one moonlight night, by an
enterprising young sportsman ; Annie was un-
fortunately drowned ; and 'Cindy fell victim to

some similar hallucination of the young son-of-a·
gun who destroyed Peter. In short, only our
old family mother-cat remained ; but, as she had
a fine litter of kittens, there was hope that :he
line would be continued. We established ner
sumptuously in a box in the back-shed with her
nurslings ; but, as cruel Fate would have it, a
marauding dog came smelling about, and a fight
ensued, in which Puss's fore-leg was broken, or,
to speak quite literally, chewed up.

Wounded and bleeding, but plucky to the last,
she drove off the dog with a "predestined
scratched face," and, taking up her kittens one
by one in her mouth, traversed a long veranda,
jumped through a window into the bed-room of
one of her mistresses, and deposited her nurslings under the bed.

All agreed that a cat of such spirit and gal-
lantry had shown that she ought to vote by her
ability to fight, and that she was at least worthy

of distinguished attention. So the next day the whole family sat in council on the case. Chloroform was administered: and, while Puss was insensible, a promising young naturalist set and bandaged the limb; but, alas! without avail. The weather was hot; and the sufferings of the poor creature soon became such, that we were thankful that we had the power, by a swift and painless death, to put an end to them. So a pistol-ball sent Puss to the land where the good cats go; and the motherless kitties found peace under the blue waters of the St. John's. The water-nymphs, undoubtedly, "held up their pearled wrists and took them in," and doubtless made blessed pets of them. So that is the end of all our cats.

Phœbus rejoices now; for there is none to molest or make him afraid. His songs increase daily in variety. He pipes and whistles; occasionally breaks forth into a litany that sounds

like "Pray do, pray do, pray do!" then, suddenly changing the stop, he shouts, "De deevil!
de deevil! de deevil!" but, as he is otherwise a
bird of the most correct habits, it cannot be
supposed that any profanity is intended. This
morning being Sunday, he called "Beecher,
Beecher, Beecher!" very volubly. He evidently is a progressive bird, and, for aught we
know, may yet express himself on some of the
questions of the day.

The next letter on our file wants to know the
prices of board at Green-Cove Springs, Magnolia, and Hibernia. The prices at these places
vary all the way from twelve to thirty-five dollars
per week, according to accommodations. The
higher prices are in larger hotels, and the
smaller in private boarding-houses. "The Florida Guide" says board can be obtained in Jacksonville, in private families, at from eight to ten
dollars per week.

There are three more letters, asking questions about the culture of the orange ; to which the writers will find answers, so far as we can give them, when we come to speak of the orange-orchards up the river.

A lady writes to ask if we know any way of preserving figs.

Practically, we know nothing about the fig-harvest, having never been here when they were ripe. Our friends tell us that they are not successful in preserving them in cans. They make a delicious though rather luscious preserve done in the ordinary way, like peaches. But we will give our inquiring friend the benefit of a piece of information communicated to us by an old native Floridian, who professed to have raised and prepared figs as fine as those in Turkey His receipt was as follows : " Prepare a lye from the ashes of the grape-vine ; have a kettle of this kept boiling hot over the fire ; throw i the figs, and let them remain two minutes ; skim them out and drain them on a sieve, and afterwards dry in the sun." Such was his receipt, which we have never tried. Probably any other strong lye would answer as well as that from the grape-vine.

As to those who have asked for flowers from Florida, we wish it were in our power to grant their requests ; but these frail beauties are not transferable. We in our colony have taxed the resources of our postal arrangements to carry to our friends small specimens, but with no very encouraging results.

We have just been making the *grand round,* or tour up the St. John's to Enterprise, across to St. Augustine, and back ; which is necessary to constitute one an accomplished Floridian sight-seer : and it had been our intention to devote this letter to that trip ; but there is so much to say, there are so many wonders and marvels to be described, that we must give it a letter by itself. No dreamland on earth can be more unearthly in its beauty and glory than the St. John's in April. Tourists, for the most part, see it only in winter, when half its gorgeous forests stand bare of leaves, and go home, never dreaming what it would be like in its resurrection-robes. So do we, in our darkness, judge the shores of the river of this mortal life up which we sail, ofttimes disappointed and complaining. We are seeing all things in winter, and not as they will be when God shall wipe away all tears, and bring about the new heavens and new earth, of which every spring is a symbol and a prophecy. The flowers and leaves of last year vanish for a season ; but they come back fresher and fairer than ever.

This bright morning we looked from the roof of our veranda, and our neighbor's oleander-trees were glowing like a great crimson cloud ; and we

said, " There! the oleanders have come back!"
No Northern ideas can give the glory of these
trees as they raise their heads in this their native
land, and seem to be covered with great crimson
roses.   The poor stunted bushes of Northern
greenhouses are   as   much   like   it   as   our
stunted virtues and poor frost-nipped enjoy-
ments shall be like the bloom and radiance of
God's paradise hereafter.   In April they begin
to bloom ; and they bloom on till November.
Language cannot do justice to the radiance,
the brightness, the celestial calm and glory,
of these spring days.   There is an assur-
ance of perpetuity in them.   You do not say, as
at the North, that a fine day is a " weather-
breeder," and expect a week of storms to pay
for it.   Day after day passes in brightness.
Morning after morning, you wake to see the same
sunshine gilding the tops of the orange-trees, and
hear the same concert of birds.   All the forest-

trees stand in perfected glory ; and the leaves have sprung forth with such rapidity and elastic vigor as gives the foliage a wondrous brightness. The black-jack oaks — trees which, for some reason or other, are apt to be spoken of as of small account — have now put forth their large, sharply-cut, oak-shaped leaves. We say this because it is the only one of the oak species here that at all resembles the oaks we have been accustomed to see. The pawpaw-bushes are all burst out in white fringes of blossom ; and the silver bells of the sparkle-berry are now in their perfection. Under foot, a whole tribe of new flowers have come in place of the departed violets. The partridge-berry or squaw-berry of the North grows in the woods in dense mats, and is now white with its little starry blossoms. Certain nameless little golden balls of flowers twinkle in the grass and leaves like small constellations. We call them, for lack of botanic language, "sun-kisses." Our party, the other night, made an expedition to the "second branch," and brought home long vines of purple wisteria, red trumpet-creeper, and some sprays of white blossoms unknown to us : so that our house still is a flower-show. Spring is as much a pomp and a glory here as in Northern States ; for although the winter is far more endurable, and preserves far more beauty, yet the outburst of vividness and vigor when the sun begins to wax powerful is even greater and more marked than at the North. The roses are now in perfection. Ours have not thriven as they might have done were it not for the all-devouring orange-trees ; but still they give us every morning, with our breakfast, a comforting assortment. La Marque, Giant of Battles, Hermosa, a little cluster rose, and a dozen more, have brightened our repast. This is the land to raise roses, however ; and we mean yet to have a rose-garden at a safe distance from any orange-trees, and see what will come of it. Here are no slugs or rose-bugs or caterpillars to make rose-culture a burden and a vexation. Finally, as we have had so many letters asking information of us, we wish somebody who is wise enough would write one, and give us some on a certain point. One of our orange-trees has become an invalid. The case may be stated as follows : Early in the season, Mr. F., in looking over the grove, found this tree, then loaded with fruit, dropping its leaves ; the leaves curling, or, as they say here, "rolling," as is the fashion of orange-trees when suffering from drought. Immediately he took all the fruit from the tree, pruned it, dug about the roots, and examined them to find something to account for this. For a while, by careful tending, the tree seemed to be coming to itself; but, when the blossoming-time came round, half its leaves fell, and it burst into blossoms on every spray and twig in the most pre-

ternatural manner.   It reminded us of some poor
dear women, who, when they lose their health,
seem resolved to kill themselves in abundant good
works.   It was really blossoming to death
Now, we ask any wise fruit-growers, What is this
disease ? and how is it to be treated ?   We have
treated it by cutting off all the blossoms, cutting
back the branches, watering with water in which
guano and lime have been dissolved ; and the
patient looks a little better.   A negro workman
testified that a tree in a similar state had been
brought back by these means.   Can any fruit-
grower give any light on this subject ?

MAGNOLIA WEEK.

IT is vain to propose and announce subjects from week to week. One must write what one is thinking of. When the mind is full of one thing, why go about to write on another?

The past week we have been engrossed by magnolias. On Monday, our friend D——, armed and equipped with scaling-ladders, ascended the glistening battlements of the great

forest palaces fronting his cottage, and bore
thence the white princesses, just bursting into
bud, and brought them down to us. Forthwith
all else was given up: for who would take the
portrait of the white lady must hurry; for, like
many queens of earth, there is but a step between perfected beauty and decay, — a moment
between beauty and ashes.

We bore them to our chamber, and before
morning the whole room was filled with the intoxicating, dreamy fragrance; and lo! while we
slept, the pearly hinges had revolved noiselessly,
and the bud that we left the evening before had
become a great and glorious flower. To de-
scend to particulars, imagine a thick, waxen-
cupped peony of the largest size, just revealing
in its centre an orange-colored cone of the size
of a walnut. Around it, like a circlet of emer-
alds, were the new green leaves, contrasting in
their vivid freshness with the solid, dark-green

brilliancy of the old foliage. The leaves of the magnolia are in themselves beauty enough without the flower. We used to gather them in a sort of rapture before we ever saw the blossom ; but all we can say of the flower is, that it is worthy of them.

We sat down before this queen of flowers, and worked assiduously at her portrait. We had, besides the full blossom, one bud of the size and shape of a large egg, which we despaired of seeing opened, but proposed to paint as it was. The second morning, our green egg began to turn forth a silver lining ; and, as we worked, we could see it slowly opening before us. Silvery and pearly were the pure tips ; while the outside was of a creamy yellow melting into green. Two days we kept faithful watch and ward at the shrine ; but, lo ! on the morning of the third our beautiful fairy had changed in the night to an ugly brownie. The petals, so waxen fair the night before, had become of a mahogany color; and a breeze passing by swept them dishonored in showers on the floor. The history of that magnolia was finished. We had seen it unfold and die. Our pearly bud, however, went on waxing and opening till its day came for full perfection.

The third day, our friend again brought in a glorious bouquet. No ordinary flower-vase would hold it. It required a heavy stone jar, and a gallon of water; but we filled the recess of our old-fashioned Franklin stove with the beauties, and the whole house was scented with their perfume.

Then we thought of the great lonely swamps and everglades where thousands of these beauties are now bursting into flower with no earthly eye to behold them.

The old German legends of female spirits inhabiting trees recurred to us. Our magnolia would make a beautiful Libussa. A flower is commonly thought the emblem of a woman; and a woman is generally thought of as something sweet, clinging, tender, and perishable. But there are women flowers that correspond to the forest magnolia, — high and strong, with a great hold of root and a great spread of branches; and whose pulsations of heart and emotion come forth like these silver lilies that illuminate the green shadows of the magnolia-forests.

Yesterday, our friend the Rev. Mr. M—— called and invited us to go with him to visit his place, situated at the mouth of Julington, just where it flows into the St. John's. Our obliging neighbor immediately proposed to take the whole party in his sailing-yacht.

An impromptu picnic was proclaimed through the house. Every one dropped the work in hand, and flew to spreading sandwiches. Oranges were gathered, luncheon-baskets

packed ; and the train filed out from the two
houses. The breeze was fresh and fair ; and
away we flew. Here, on the St. John's, a water-
coach is more to the purpose, in the present
state of our wood-roads, than any land-carriage ;
and the delight of sailing is something infi-
nitely above any other locomotion. On this
great, beautiful river you go drifting like a
feather or a cloud ; while the green, fragrant
shores form a constantly-varying picture as you
pass. Yesterday, as we were sailing, we met a
little green, floating island, which seemed to
have started out on its own account, and gone to
seek its fortune. We saw it at first in the distance, — a small, undulating spot of vivid green.
Our little craft was steered right alongside, so
that we could minutely observe. It was some
half-dozen square yards of pickerel-weed, bonnet
water-lettuce, and other water-plants, which, it
would seem, had concluded to colonize, and go

out to see the world in company. We watched them as they went nodding and tilting off over the blue waters, and wondered where they would bring up.

But now we are at the mouth of Julington, and running across to a point of land on the other side. Our boat comes to anchor under a grove of magnolia-trees which lean over the water. They are not yet fully in blossom. One lily-white bud and one full-blown flower appear on a low branch overhanging the river, and are marked to be gathered when we return. We go up, and begin strolling along the shore. The magnolia-grove extends along the edge of the water for half a mile. Very few flowers are yet developed; but the trees themselves, in the vivid contrast of the new leaves with the old, are beauty enough. Out of the centre of the spike of last year's solemn green comes the most vivid, varnished cluster of fresh young leaves,

and from the centre of this brilliant cluster
comes the flower-bud. The magnolia, being an
evergreen, obeys in its mode of growth the law
which governs all evergreens. When the new
shoots come out, the back-leaves fall off. This
produces in the magnolia a wonderfully-beauti-
ful effect of color. As we looked up in the
grove, each spike had, first, the young green
leaves ; below those, the dark, heavy ones ; and
below those still, the decaying ones, preparing to
fall. These change with all the rich colors of
decaying leaves. Some are of a pure, brilliant
yellow ; others yellow, mottled and spotted with
green ; others take a tawny orange, and again a
faded brown.

The afternoon sun, shining through this grove,
gave all these effects of color in full brightness.
The trees, as yet, had but here and there a blossom. Each shoot had its bud, for the most part
no larger than a walnut. The most advanced

were of the size of an egg, of white tinted with
green. Beneath the trees the ground was
thickly strewn with the golden brown and
mottled leaves, which were ever and anon sailing down as the wind swayed them.

Numbers of little seedling magnolias were
springing up everywhere about us ; and we easily
pulled up from the loose yielding soil quite a
number of them, wrapping their roots in the
gray moss which always lies at hand for packing-
purposes.

The place had many native wild orange-trees,
which had been cut off and budded with the
sweet orange, and were making vigorous
growth. Under the shade of the high live-oaks
Mr. M—— had set out young orange and
lemon trees through quite an extent of the
forest. He told us that he had two thousand
plants thus growing. It is becoming a favorite
idea with fruit-planters here, that the tropical

fruits are less likely to be injured by frosts, and make a more rapid and sure growth, under the protecting shadow of live-oaks. The wild orange is found frequently growing in this way; and they take counsel of Nature in this respect.

After wandering a while in the wood, we picnicked under a spreading live-oak, with the breeze from the river drawing gratefully across us.

Our dinner over, Mr. M—— took us through his plantations of grapes, peaches, and all other good things. Black Hamburg grapes grafted upon the root of the native vine had made luxuriant growth, and were setting full of grapes. There were shoots of this year's growth full six and seven feet in length. In the peach-orchard were trees covered with young peaches, which Mr. M—— told us were only three years from the seed. All the garden vegetables were there in fine order; and the string-beans appeared to be in full maturity.

It is now five years since Mr. M—— bought and began to clear this place, then a dense forest. At first, the letting-in of the sun on the decaying vegetation, and the upturning of the soil, made the place unhealthy ; and it was found necessary to remove the family. Now the work is done, the place cleared, and, he says, as healthy as any other.

Mr. M—— is an enthusiastic horticulturist and florist, and is about to enrich the place with a rose-garden of some thousands of choice varieties. These places in Florida must not in any wise be compared with the finished ones of Northern States. They are spots torn out of the very heart of the forest, and where Nature is rebelling daily, and rushing with all her might back again into the wild freedom from which she has been a moment led captive.

But a day is coming when they will be wonderfully beautiful and productive.

We had one adventure in conquering and killing a formidable-looking black-snake about seven feet in length. He had no fangs, and, Mr. M—— told us, belonged to a perfectly respectable and harmless family, whose only vice is chicken-stealing. They are called chicken-snakes, in consequence of the partiality they show for young chickens, which they swallow, feathers and all, with good digestion and relish. He informed us that they were vigorous ratters, and better than either terrier or cat for keeping barns clear of rats ; and that for this purpose they were often cherished in granaries, as they will follow the rats to retreats where cats cannot go. Imagine the feelings of a rat when this dreadful visitor comes like grim death into his family-circle !

In regard to snakes in general, the chance of meeting hurtful ones in Florida is much less than in many other States. Mr. M——, who in the way of his mission has ridden all through Florida, never yet met a rattlesnake, or was endangered by any venomous serpent. Perhaps the yearly burnings of the grass which have been practised so long in Florida have had some effect in checking the increase of serpents by destroying their eggs.

As the afternoon sun waxed low we sought our yacht again, and came back with two magnolia-flowers and several buds.

This week, too, the woods are full of the blossoms of the passion-flower.

Our neighbor Mr. C—— has bought the beautiful oak-hammock, where he is preparing to build a house. Walking over to see the spot the other evening, we found a jungle of passion-flowers netted around on the ground, and clinging to bush and tree. Another neighbor also brought us in some branches of a flowering-shrub called the Indian pipe, which eclipses the sparkleberry. Like that, it seems to be a glorified variety of high huckleberry or blueberry. It has the greatest profusion of waxen white bells fringing every twig; and, *blasé* as we have been with floral displays, we had a new sensation when it was brought into the house.

Thus goes the floral procession in April in the wild-woods. In the gardens, the oleanders, pink, white, and deep crimson, are beginning their long season of bloom. The scarlet pomegranate, with its vivid sparks of color, shines through the leaves.

We are sorry for all those who write to beg that we will send by mail a specimen of this or that flower. Our experience has shown us that in that way they are *not* transferable. Magnolia-buds would arrive dark and dreadful; and it is far better to view the flowers ever fresh and blooming, through imagination, than to receive a desolate, faded, crumpled remnant by mail.

BUYING LAND IN FLORIDA.

WE have before us a neat little pile of what we call "Palmetto letters," — responses to our papers from all States in the Union. Our knowledge of geography has really been quite brightened by the effort to find out where all our correspondents are living. Nothing could more mark the exceptional severity of the recent winter than the bursts of enthusiasm with which the tidings of flowers

and open-air freedom in Florida have come to
those struggling through snow-drifts and hail-
storms in the more ungenial parts of our Union.
Florida seems to have risen before their vision
as the hymn sings of better shores : —

> " On Jordan's stormy banks I stand,
>   And cast a wistful eye
>   To Canaan's fair and happy land."

Consequently, the letters of inquiry have
come in showers. What is the price of land?
Where shall we go? How shall we get there?
&c.

We have before advertised you, O beloved
unknown! who write, that your letters are welcome, ofttimes cheering, amusing, and undenia-
bly nice letters; yet we cannot pledge ourselves
to answer, except in the gross, and through " The
Christian Union." The last inquiry is from
three brothers, who want to settle and have

homes together at the South. They ask, "Is there government land that can be had in Florida?' Yes, there is a plenty of it; yet, as Florida is the oldest settled State in the Union, and has always been a sort of bone for which adventurers have wrangled, the best land in it has been probably taken up. We do not profess to be land-agents; and we speak only for the tract of land lying on the St. John's River, between Mandarin and Jacksonville, when we say that there are thousands of acres of good land, near to a market, near to a great river on which three or four steamboats are daily plying, that can be had for five dollars per acre, and for even less than that. Fine, handsome building-lots in the neighborhood of Jacksonville are rising in value, commanding much higher prices than the mere productive value of the land. In other words, men pay for advantages, for society, for facilities afforded by settlements.

Now, for the benefit of those who are seriously thinking of coming to Florida, we have
taken some pains to get the practical experience
of men who are now working the land, as to
what it will do. On the 2d of May, we
accepted the invitation of Col. Hardee to visit
his pioneer nursery, now in the fourth year of
its existence. Mr. Hardee is an enthusiast in
his business ; and it is a department where we
are delighted to see enthusiasm. The close of
the war found him, as he said, miserably poor.
But, brave and undiscouraged, he retained his
former slaves as free laborers ; took a tract of
land about a mile and a half from Jacksonville ;
put up a house ; cleared, planted, ploughed, and
digged : and, in the course of four years, results
are beginning to tell handsomely, as they always
do for energy and industry. He showed us
through his grounds, where every thing was
growing at the rate things do grow here in the

month of May. Two things Mr. Hardee seems
to have demonstrated: first, that strawberry-
culture may be a success in Florida; and,
second, that certain varieties of Northern apples
and pears may be raised here. We arrived in
Florida in the middle of January; and one of
the party who spent a night at the St. James
was surprised by seeing a peck of fresh, ripe
strawberries brought in. They were from Mr.
Hardee's nursery, and grown in the open air;
and he informed us that they had, during all the
winter, a daily supply of the fruit, sufficient for a
large family, and a considerable overplus for the
market. The month of May, however, is the
height of the season; and they were picking,
they informed us, at the rate of eighty quarts
per day.

In regard to apples and pears, Mr. Hardee's
method is to graft them upon the native haw-
thorn; and the results are really quite wonder-

ful. Mr. Hardee was so complaisant as to cut
and present to us a handsome cluster of red
Astrachan apples about the size of large hickory-
nuts, the result of the second year from the graft.
Several varieties of pears had made a truly
astonishing growth, and promise to fruit, in time,
abundantly. A large peach-orchard presented
a show of peaches, some of the size of a butter-
nut, and some of a walnut. Concerning one
which he called the Japan peach, he had san-
guine hope of ripe fruit in ten days. We were
not absolute in the faith as to the exact date,
but believe that there will undoubtedly be ripe
peaches there before the month of May is out.
Mr. Hardee is particularly in favor of cultivating
fruit in partially-shaded ground. Most of these
growths we speak of were under the shade of
large live-oaks; but when he took us into the
wild forest, and showed us peach, orange, and
lemon trees set to struggle for existence on the

same footing, and with only the same advantages, as the wild denizens of the forest, we rather demurred. Was not this pushing theory to extremes? Time will show.

Col. Hardee has two or three native seedling peaches grown in Florida, of which he speaks highly, — Mrs. Thompson's Golden Free, which commences ripening in June, and continues till the first of August; the "Cracker Cart," very large, weighing sometimes thirteen ounces; the Cling Yellow; and the Japan, very small and sweet, ripening in May.

Besides these, Mr. Hardee has experimented largely in vines, in which he gives preference to the Isabella, Hartford Prolific, and Concord.

He is also giving attention to roses and ornamental shrubbery. What makes the inception of such nurseries as Mr. Hardee's a matter of congratulation is that they furnish to purchasers things that have been proved suited to the climate and soil of Florida. Peach-trees, roses, and grapes, sent from the North, bring here the habit of their Northern growth, which often makes them worthless. With a singular stubbornness, they adhere to the times and seasons to which they have been accustomed farther North. We set a peach-orchard of some four hundred trees which we obtained from a nursery in Georgia. We suspect now, that, having a press of orders, our nurseryman simply sent us a packet of trees from some Northern nursery. The consequence is, that year after year, when all nature about them is bursting into leaf and blossom, when peaches of good size gem the boughs of Florida trees, our peach-orchard stands sullen and leafless; nor will it start bud or blossom till the time for peaches to start in New York. The same has been our trouble with some fine varieties of roses which we took from our Northern grounds. As yet, they are hardly worth the ground they occupy; and whether they ever will do any thing is a matter of doubt. Meanwhile we have only to ride a little way into the pine-woods to see around many a rustic cabin a perfect blaze of crimson roses and cluster roses, foaming over the fences in cascades of flowers. These are Florida roses, born and bred; and this is the way they do with not one tithe of the work and care that we have expended on our poor Northern exiles. Mr. Hardee, therefore, in attempting the pioneer nursery of Florida, is doing a good thing for every new-comer; and we wish him all success. As a parting present, we received a fine summer squash, which, for the first of May, one must admit is good growth. And now, for the benefit of those who may want to take up land in Florida, we shall give the experience of some friends and neighbors of ours who have carried through about as thorough and well-conducted an experiment as any ; and we give it from memoranda which they have kindly furnished, in the hope of being of use to other settlers.

OUR EXPERIENCE IN CROPS.

 FEW years ago, three brothers, farmers, from Vermont, exhausted by the long, hard winters there, came to Florida to try an experiment. They bought two hundred and seventy-five acres in the vicinity of Mandarin at one dollar per acre. It was pineland, that had been cut over twice for timber, and was now considered of no further value by its possessor, who threw it into the hands of a land-agent to make what he could of it. It was the very cheapest kind of Florida land.

Of this land they cleared only thirty-five acres. The fencing cost two hundred dollars. They put up a large, unplastered, two-story house, with piazzas to both floors, at a cost of about a thousand dollars. The additional outlay was on two mules and a pair of oxen, estimated at four hundred dollars. The last year, they put up a sugar-mill and establishment at a cost of five hundred dollars.

An orange-grove, a vineyard, and a peach-orchard, are all included in the programme of these operators, and are all well under way. But these are later results. It is not safe to calculate on an orange-grove under ten years, or on a vineyard or peach-orchard under four or five.

We have permission to copy *verbatim* certain memoranda of results with which they have furnished us.

CABBAGES.

First Year. — Sowed seed in light sandy soil without manure. Weak plants, beaten down by rain, lost.

Second Year. — Put out an acre and a half of fine plants: large part turned out poorly. Part of the land was low, sour, and wet, and all meagrely fertilized. Crop sold in Jacksonville for two hundred and fifty dollars.

Third Year. — Three acres better, but still inadequately manured, and half ruined by the Christmas frost: brought about eight hundred dollars.

Fourth Year (1871–72.) — Two acres better manured ; planted in low land, on ridges five feet apart : returned six hundred dollars. In favorable seasons, with good culture, an acre of cabbages should yield a gross return of five hundred dollars, of which three hundred would be clear profit.

CUCUMBERS

First Year. — Planted four acres, mostly new, hard, sour land, broad-casting fifty bushels of lime to the acre, and using some weak, half-rotted compost in the hills : wretched crop. The whole lot sent North : did not pay for shipment.

Second Year. — An acre and a half best land, heavily manured with well-rotted compost worked into drills eight feet apart : yielded fifty bushels, which brought two hundred and fifty dollars in New York. More would have been realized, except that an untimely hail-storm spoiled the vines prematurely.

Third Year. — An acre and a half, well cul-· tivated and manured, yielded four hundred bushels, and brought a gross return of thirteen hundred dollars.

TOMATOES.

First Year. — Lost many plants through rain and wet, and insufficient manure. Those we got to the New-York market brought from four to six dollars per bushel.

Second Year. — Manured too heavily in the hill with powerful unfermented manures. A heavy rain helped ruin the crop. Those, however, which we sent to market, brought good prices.

Third Year. — None planted for market ; but those for family use did so well as to put us in good humor with the crop, and induce us to plant for this year.

SWEET-POTATOES.

Every year we have had pretty good success with them on land well prepared with lime and ashes. We have had three hundred and fifty bushels to the acre.

SUGAR-CANE

Has done very respectably on one-year-old soil manured with ashes only ; while mellow land, well prepared with muck, ashes, and fish-guano, has yielded about twenty barrels of sugar to the acre.

IRISH POTATOES.

We have found these on light soil, with only moderate fertilizing, an unprofitable crop at four dollars, but on good land, with very heavy manuring, decidedly profitable at two dollars per bushel. Fine potatoes rarely are less than that in Jacksonville. They will be ready to dig in April and May.

PEAS

May be extraordinarily profitable, and may fail entirely. A mild winter, without severe frosts, would bring them early into market. The

Christmas freeze of 1870 caught a half-acre of our peas in blossom, and killed them to the ground.

Planted in the latter part of January, both peas and potatoes are pretty sure. We have not done much with peas; but a neighbor of ours prefers them to cabbages. He gets about three dollars per bushel.

As a general summary, our friend adds, —

" For two years in succession, we have found our leading market-crops handsomely remunerative. The net returns look well compared with those of successful gardening near New York. Cabbages raised here during the fall and winter, without any protection, bear as good price as do the spring cabbages which are raised in cold-frames at the North; and early cucumbers, grown in the open air, have been worth as much to us as to Northern gardeners who have grown them in hot-beds.

" The secret of our success is an open one ; but we ourselves do not yet come up to our mark, and reduce our preaching to practice.   We have hardly made a good beginning in high manuring. We did not understand at first, as we now do, the difference between ordinary crops and *early* vegetables and fruits.   Good corn may be raised on poor land at the rate of five or ten bushels to the acre ; but, on a hundred acres of scantily-fertilized land, scarcely a single handsome cabbage can be grown.   So with cucumbers : they will neither be early, nor fit for market, if raised on ordinary land with ordinary culture.   Most of the market-gardening in Florida, so far as we know it, cannot but prove disastrous.   Land-agents and visionaries hold forth that great crops may be expected from insignificant outlays ; and so they decoy the credulous to their ruin.   To undertake raising vegetables in Florida, with these ideas of low culture, is to embark in a leaky and surely-sinking ship. If one is unwilling to expend for manure alone upon a single acre in one year enough to buy a hundred acres of new land, let him give a wide berth to market-gardening. Such expenditures have to be met at the North ; and there is no getting round it at the South.

"Yet one can economize here as one cannot at the North. The whole culture of an early vegetable-garden can go on in connection with the later crop of sugar-cane. Before our cabbages were off the ground this spring, we had our cane-rows between them ; and we never before prepared the ground and planted the cane so easily. On another field we have the cane-rows eight feet apart, and tomatoes and snap-beans intervening. We have suffered much for lack of proper drainage. We have actually lost enough from water standing upon crops to have underdrained the whole enclosure. We undertook to till more acres than we could do justice to. In farming, the *love of acres* is the root of all evil."

So much for our friend's experiences. We consider this experiment a most valuable one for all who contemplate buying land and settling in Florida. It is an experiment in which untiring industry, patience, and economy have been brought into exercise. It has been tried on the very cheapest land in Florida, and its results are most instructive.

Market-gardening must be the immediate source of support; and therefore this experiment is exactly in point.

This will show that the land is the least of the expense in starting a farm ; and that it is best, in the first instance, to spend little for land, and much for the culture of it.

Thousands of people pour down into Florida to winter, and must be fed. The Jacksonville market, and the markets of all the different boarding establishments on the river, need ample supplies ; and there is no fear that there will not be a ready sale for all that could be raised.

Our friends are willing to make a free contribution of their own failures and mistakes for the good of those who come after. It shows that a new country must be *studied* and tried before success is attained. New-comers, by settling in the vicinity of successful planters, may shorten the painful paths of experience.

All which we commend to all those who have written to inquire about buying *land* in Florida.

MAY IN FLORIDA.

MANDARIN, May 28, 1872.

HE month of May in Florida corresponds to July and August at the north.

Strawberries, early peaches, blackberries, huckleberries, blueberries, and two species of wild plums, are the fruits of this month, and make us forget to want the departing oranges. Still, however, some of these cling to the bough ; and it is astonishing how juicy and refreshing they still are. The blueberries are larger and sweeter, and less given to hard seeds, than any we have ever tasted. In the way of garden-vegetables, summer squashes, string-beans, and tomatoes are fully in season.

This year, for the most part, the month has been most delightful weather.

With all the pomp and glory of Nature in full view; beholding in the wet, low lands red, succulent shoots, which, under the moist, fiery breath of the season, seem really to grow an inch at a time, and to shoot up as by magic ; hearing bird-songs filling the air from morning to night, — we feel a sort of tropical exultation, as if great, succulent shoots of passion or poetry might spring up within us from out this growing dream-life.

The birds ! — who can describe their jubilees, their exultations, their never-ending, still beginning babble and jargon of sweet sounds ? All day the air rings with sweet fanciful trills and

melodies, as if there were a thousand little vibrat-
ing bells.   They iterate and reiterate one sweet
sound after another ; they call to one another,
and answer from thicket to thicket ; they pipe ;
they whistle ; they chatter and mock at each
other with airy defiance : and sometimes it seems
as if the very air broke into rollicking bird-
laughter.   A naturalist, who, like Thoreau, has
sojourned for months in the Florida forests to
study and observe Nature, has told us that no
true idea of the birds' plumage can be got till
the hot months come on.   Then the sun pours
light and color, and makes feathers like steely
armor.

The birds love the sun : they adore him.
Our own Phœbus, when his cage is hung on the
shady side of the veranda, hangs sulky and
silent ; but put him in the full blaze of the
sun, and while the thermometer is going up to
the nineties, he rackets in a perfectly crazy

abandon of bird babblement, singing all he ever heard before, and trying his bill at new notes, and, as a climax, ending each outburst with a purr of satisfaction like an overgrown cat. Several pairs of family mocking-birds have their nests somewhere in our orange-trees ; and there is no end of amusement in watching their dainty evolutions. Sometimes, for an hour at a time, one of them, perched high and dry on a topmost twig, where he gets the full blaze of the sun, will make the air ring with so many notes and noises, that it would seem as if he were forty birds instead of one. Then, again, you will see him stealing silently about as if on some mysterious mission, perching here and there with a peculiar nervous jerk of his long tail, and a silent little lift of his wings, as if he were fanning himself. What this motion is for, we have never been able to determine.

Our plantation, at present, is entirely given

over to the domestic affairs of the mocking-birds, dozens of whom have built their nests in the green, inaccessible fastnesses of the orange-trees, and been rearing families in security. Now, however, the young birds are to be taught to fly; and the air resounds with the bustle and chatter of the operation. Take, for example, one scene which is going on as we write. Down on the little wharf which passes through the swamp in front of our house, three or four juvenile mocking-birds are running up and down like chickens, uttering plaintive cries of distress. On either side, perched on a tall, dry, last-year's coffee-bean-stalk, sit ' papa and mamma," chattering, scolding, exhorting, and coaxing. The little ones run from side to side, and say in plaintive squeaks, "I can't," "I daren't," as plain as birds can say it. There! now they spread their little wings; and — oh, joy! — they find to their delight that they do not fall: they exult in the possession of a new-born sense of existence. As we look at this pantomime, graver thoughts come over us, and we think how poor, timid little souls moan, and hang back, and tremble, when the time comes to leave this nest of earth, and trust themselves to the free air of the world they were made for. As the little bird's moans and cries end in delight and rapture in finding himself in a new, glorious, free life; so, just beyond the dark step of death, will come a buoyant, exulting sense of new existence. Our life here is in intimate communion with bird-life. Their singing all day comes in bursts and snatches; and one awakes to a sort of wondering consciousness of the many airy dialects with which the blue heavens are filled. At night a whippoorwill or two, perched in the cypress-trees, make a plaintive and familiar music. When the nights are hot, and the moon bright, the mocking-birds burst into gushes of song at any hour. At mid-

night we have risen to listen to them. Birds
are as plenty about us as chickens in a barn-
yard; and one wonders at their incessant activity
and motion, and studies what their quaint little
fanciful ways may mean, half inclined to say
with Cowper, —

> " But I, whatever powers were mine,
>   Would cheerfully those gifts resign
>   For such a pair of wings as thine,
>   And such a head between 'em."

Speaking of birds reminds us of a little pas-
toral which is being enacted in the neighborhood of St. Augustine. A young man from
Massachusetts, driven to seek health in a milder
climate, has bought a spot of land for a nursery-
garden in the neighborhood of St. Augustine.
We visited his place, and found him and his
mother in a neat little cottage, adorned only
with grasses and flowers picked in the wild

woods, and living in perfect familiarity with the
birds, which they have learned to call in from
the neighboring forests. It has become one of
the fashionable amusements in the season for
strangers to drive out to this cottage and see the
birds fed. At a cry from the inmates of the
cottage, the blue-jays and mocking-birds will
come in flocks, settle on their shoulders, eat out
of their hands, or out of the hands of any one
who chooses to hold food to them. When we
drove out, however, the birds were mostly dis-
persed about their domestic affairs ; this being
the nesting season. Moreover, the ample supply of fresh wild berries in the woods makes
them less anxious for such dry food as contented
them in winter. Only one pet mocking-bird
had established himself in a neighboring tree,
and came at their call. Pic sat aloft, switching
his long tail with a jerky air of indifference, like
an *enfant gâté*. When raisins were thrown up,

he caught them once or twice ; but at last, with an evident bird-yawn, declared that it was no go, and he didn't care for raisins.　Ungrateful Pic ! Next winter, eager and hungry, he will be grateful ; and so with all the rest of them.

One of the charms of May not to be forgotten is the blossoming of the great Cape jessamine that stands at the end of the veranda, which has certainly had as many as three or four hundred great, white, fragrant flowers at once.

As near as possible, this is the most perfect of flowers.　It is as pure as the white camellia, with the added gift of exquisite perfume.　It is a camellia with a soul !　Its leaves are of most brilliant varnished green ; its buds are lovely ; and its expanded flower is of a thick, waxen texture, and as large as a large camellia.　We have sat moonlight nights at the end of the veranda, and enjoyed it.　It wraps one in an atmosphere of perfume.　Only one fault has this bush : it blossoms only once a season ; not, like the ever-springing oleander, for months. One feels a sense of hurry to enjoy and appropriate a bloom so rare, that lasts only a few weeks.

Here in Florida, flowers form a large item of thought and conversation wherever one goes ; and the reason of it is the transcendent beauty and variety that are here presented. We have just returned from St. Augustine, and seen some gardens where wealth and leisure have expended themselves on flowers ; and in our next chapter we will tell of some of these beauties.

ST. AUGUSTINE.

MANDARIN, May 30, 1872.

HE thermometer with us, during the third week in May, rose to ninety-two in the shade ; and as we had received an invitation from a friend to visit St. Augustine, which is the Newport of Florida, we thought it a good time to go seaward. So on a pleasant morning we embarked on the handsome boat "Florence," which has taken so many up the river, and thus secured all the breeze that was to be had.

"The Florence" is used expressly for a river pleasure-boat, plying every day between Jacksonville and Pilatka. It is long and airy, and nicely furnished; and one could not imagine a more delightful conveyance. In hot weather, one could not be more sure of cool breezes than when sailing up and down perpetually in "The Florence." Our destiny, however, landed us in the very meridian of the day at Tekoi. Tekoi consists of a shed and a sand-bank, and a little shanty, where, to those who require, refreshments are served.

On landing, we found that we must pay for the pleasure and coolness of coming up river in "The Florence" by waiting two or three mortal hours till "The Starlight" arrived; for the railroad-car would not start till the full complement of passengers was secured. We had a good opportunity then of testing what the heat of a Florida sun might be, untempered by live-oaks and orange shades, and unalleviated by ice-water; and the lesson was an impressive one.

The railroad across to St. Augustine is made of wooden rails; and the cars are drawn by horses.

There was one handsome car like those used on the New-York horse-railroads: the others were the roughest things imaginable. Travellers have usually spoken of this road with execration for its slowness and roughness; but over this, such as it was, all the rank and fashion of our pleasure-seekers, the last winter, have been pouring in unbroken daily streams. In the height of the season, when the cars were crowded, four hours were said to be consumed in performing this fifteen miles. We, however, did it in about two.

To us this bit of ride through the Florida

woods is such a never-ceasing source of interest and pleasure, that we do not mind the slowness of it, and should regret being whisked by at steam-speed. We have come over it three times ; and each time the varieties of shrubs and flowers, grasses and curious leaves, were a never-failing study and delight. Long reaches of green moist land form perfect flower-gardens, whose variety of bloom changes with every month. The woods hang full of beautiful climbing plants. The coral honeysuckle and the red bignonia were in season now. Through glimpses and openings here and there we could see into forests of wild orange-trees ; and palmetto-palms raised their scaly trunks and gigantic green fans. The passengers could not help admiring the flowers : and as there were many stops and pauses, and as the gait of the horses was never rapid, it was quite easy for the gentlemen to gather and bring in specimens of all the beau-

14

ties ; and the flowers formed the main staple of the conversation. They were so very bright and gay and varied, that even the most unobserving could not but notice them.

St. Augustine stands on a flat, sandy level, encompassed for miles and miles by what is called " scrub," — a mixture of low palmettoes and bushes of various descriptions. Its history carries one back almost to the middle ages. For instance, Menendez, who figured as commandant in its early day, was afterwards appointed to command the Spanish Armada, away back in the times of Queen Elizabeth ; but, owing to the state of his health, he did not accept the position.

In the year 1586, Elizabeth then being at war with Spain, her admiral, Sir Francis Drake, bombarded St. Augustine, and took it ; helping himself, among other things, to seven brass cannon, two thousand pounds in money, and other booty. In 1605 it was taken and plundered by buccaneers; in 1702, besieged by the people of the Carolinas; in 1740, besieged again by Gen. Oglethorpe of Georgia.

So we see that this part of our country, at least, does not lie open to the imputation so often cast upon America, of having no historic associations; though, like a great deal of the world's history, it is written in letters of blood and fire.

Whoever would know, let him read Parkman's "Pioneers of France," under the article "Huguenots in Florida," and he will see how the first Spanish governor, Menendez, thought he did God service when he butchered in cold blood hundreds of starving, shipwrecked Huguenots who threw themselves on his mercy, and to whom he had extended pledges of shelter and protection.

A government-officer, whose ship is stationed

in Matanzas Inlet, told me that the tradition is that the place is still haunted by the unquiet ghosts of the dead. An old negro came to him, earnestly declaring that he had heard often, at midnight, shrieks and moans, and sounds as of expostulation, and earnest cries in some foreign language, at that place ; and that several white people whom he had taken to the spot had heard the same. On inquiring of his men, Capt. H—— could find none who had heard the noises ; although, in digging in the sands, human bones were often disinterred. But surely, by all laws of demonology, here is where there ought to be the materials for a first-class ghost-story. Here, where there has been such crime, cruelty, treachery, terror, fear, and agony, we might fancy mourning shades wandering in unrest, — shades of the murderers, forever deploring their crime and cruelty.

The aspect of St. Augustine is quaint and

strange, in harmony with its romantic history. It has no pretensions to architectural richness or beauty ; and yet it is impressive from its unlikeness to any thing else in America. It is as if some little, old, dead-and-alive Spanish town, with its fort and gateway and Moorish bell-towers, had broken loose, floated over here, and got stranded on a sand-bank. Here you see the shovel-hats and black gowns of priests ; the convent, with gliding figures of nuns ; and in the narrow, crooked streets meet dark-browed people with great Spanish eyes and coal-black hair. The current of life here has the indolent, dreamy stillness that characterizes life in Old Spain. In Spain, when you ask a man to do any thing, instead of answering as we do, " In a minute," the invariable reply is, " In an hour ; " and the growth and progress of St. Augustine have been according. There it stands, alone, isolated, connected by no good roads or naviga-

tion with the busy, living world.   Before 1835,
St. Augustine was a bower of orange-trees.
Almost every house looked forth from these en-
circling shades.   The frost came and withered
all ; and in very few cases did it seem to come
into the heads of the inhabitants to try again.
The orange-groves are now the exception, not
the rule ; and yet for thirty years it has been
quite possible to have them.

As the only seaport city of any size in
Florida, St. Augustine has many attractions.
Those who must choose a Southern home, and
who are so situated that they must remain
through the whole summer in the home of their
choice, could not do better than to choose St.
Augustine.   It is comparatively free from malarial fevers ; and the sea-air tempers the oppressive heats of summer, so that they are quite
endurable.   Sea-bathing can be practised in
suitable bathing-houses ; but the sharks make

open sea-bathing dangerous. If one comes expecting a fine view of the open ocean, however, one will be disappointed; for Anastasia Island — a long, low sand-bar — stretches its barren line across the whole view, giving only so much sea-prospect as can be afforded by the arm of the sea — about two miles wide — which washes the town. Little as this may seem of the ocean, the town lies so flat and low, that, in stormy weather, the waves used to be driven up into it, so as to threaten its destruction. A sea-wall of solid granite masonry was deemed necessary to secure its safety, and has been erected by the United-States Government. This wall affords a favorite promenade to the inhabitants, who there enjoy good footing and sea-breezes.

What much interested us in St. Augustine was to see the results of such wealth and care as are expended at the North on gardening being brought to bear upon gardens in this

semi-tropical region. As yet, all that we have
seen in Florida has been the beginning of industrial experiments, where utility has been the
only thing consulted, and where there has been
neither time nor money to seek the ornamental.
Along the St. John's you can see, to-day, hundreds of places torn from the forest, yet showing the unrotted stumps of the trees ; the house
standing in a glare of loose white sand, in
which one sinks over shoes at every step. If
there be a flower-garden (and, wherever there is
a woman, there will be), its prospects in the loose
sliding sands appear discouraging. Boards and
brick-edgings are necessary to make any kind
of boundaries ; and a man who has to cut down a
forest, dig a well, build a house, plant an orange-
grove, and meanwhile raise enough garden-stuff
to pay his way, has small time for the graces.

But here in St. Augustine are some families
of wealth and leisure, driven to seek such a

winter-home, who amuse themselves during their stay in making that home charming ; and the results are encouraging.

In the first place, the slippery sand-spirit has been caught, and confined under green grass-plats. The grass problem has been an earnest study with us ever since we came here. What grass will bear a steady blaze of the sun for six months, with the thermometer at a hundred and thirty or forty, is a question. It is perfectly easy, as we have proved by experiment, to raise flattering grass-plats of white clover, and even of the red-top, during the cool, charming months of January, February, and March ; but their history will be summed up in the scriptural account — " which to day is, and to-morrow is cast into the oven " — as soon as May begins.

The chances of an enduring sod for ornamental purposes are confined to two varieties, — the broad and the narrow leafed Bermuda grasses.

These have roots that run either to the centre of the earth, or far enough in that direction for practical purposes; and are, besides, endowed with the faculty of throwing out roots at every joint, so that they spread rapidly. The broad-leafed kind is what is principally employed in St. Augustine; and we have seen beautifully-kept gardens where it is cut into borders, and where the grass-plats and croquet-grounds have been made of it to admirable advantage. A surface of green in this climate is doubly precious to the eye.

We were visiting in a house which is a model for a hot climate. A wide, cool hall runs through the centre; and wide verandas, both above and below, go around the whole four sides. From these we could look down at our leisure into the foliage of a row of Magnolia grandiflora, now in blossom. Ivy, honey-suckles, manrundia, and a host of other

climbing - plants, make a bower of these outside corridors of the house. The calla-lilies
blossom almost daily in shaded spots ; and beds
of fragrant blue violets are never without
flowers. Among the ornamental shrubbery we
noticed the chaparral, — a thorny tree, with
clusters of yellow blossoms, and long, drooping,
peculiar leaves, resembling in effect the willow-
leafed acacia. The banana has a value simply
as an ornamental-leaf plant, quite apart from the
consideration of its fruit, which one can buy, perhaps, better than one can raise, in this part of
Florida; but it is glorious, when the thermometer
is going up into the hundreds, to see the great,
fresh, broad, cool leaves of the banana-tree leap-
ing into life, and seeming to joy in existence. In
groups of different sizes, they form most beautiful and effective shrubbery. The secret of
gardening well here is to get things that love
the sun. Plants that come originally from hot

regions, and that rejoice the hotter it grows, are those to be sought for. The date-palm has many beautiful specimens in the gardens of St. Augustine. A date-palm, at near view, is as quaint and peculiar a specimen of Nature as one can imagine. Its trunk seems built up of great scales, in which ferns and vines root themselves, and twine and ramble, and hang in festoons. Above, the leaves, thirty feet long, fall in a feathery arch, and in the centre, like the waters of a fountain, shoot up bright, yellow, drooping branches that look like coral. These are the flower-stalks. The fruit, in this climate, does not ripen so as to be good for any thing.

One gentleman showed me a young palm, now six feet high, which he had raised from a seed of the common shop date, planted four years ago. In this same garden he showed me enormous rose-trees, which he had formed by budding the finest of the Bourbon ever-blooming roses in the native Florida rose. The growth in three years had been incredible ; and these trees are an ever-springing fountain of fresh roses. There is a rose-tree in St. Augustine, in a little garden, which all the sight-seers go to see. It is a tree with a trunk about the size of an ordinary man's arm, and is said to have had a thousand roses on it at a time. Half that number will answer our purpose ; and we will set it down at that. Rose-slugs and rose-bugs are pests unheard of here. The rose grows as in its native home. One very pretty feature of the houses here struck me agreeably. There is oftentimes a sort of shaded walk under half the house, opening upon the garden. You go up a dusty street, and stand at a door, which you expect will open into a hall. It opens, and a garden full of flowers and trees meets your view. The surprise is delightful. In one garden that we visited we saw a century-plant in bud. The stalk was nineteen feet high ; and the blossoms seemed to promise to be similar to those of the yucca. The leaves are like the aloe, only longer, and twisted and contorted in a strange, weird fashion. On the whole, it looked as if it might have been one of the strange plants in Rappicini's garden in Padua.

The society in St. Augustine, though not extensive, is very delightful. We met and were introduced to some very cultivated, agreeable people. There is a fair prospect that the city will soon be united by railroad to Jacksonville, which will greatly add to the facility and convenience of living there. We recrossed the railroad at Tekoi, on our way home, in company with a party of gentlemen who are investigating that road with a view of putting capital into it, and so getting it into active running order. One of them informed me. that he was also going to Indian River to explore, in view of the projected plan to unite it with the St. John's by means of a canal. Very sensibly he remarked, that, in order to really make up one's mind about Florida, one should see it in summer ; to which we heartily assented.

By all these means this beautiful country is being laid open, and made accessible and inhabitable as a home and refuge for those who need it.

On the steamboat, coming back, we met the Florida Thoreau of whom we before spoke, — a devoted, enthusiastic lover of Nature as she reveals herself in the most secluded everglades and forests. He supports himself, and pays the expenses of his tours, by selling the curiosities of Nature which he obtains to the crowd of eager visitors who throng the hotels in winter. The feathers of the pink curlew, the heron, the crane, the teeth of alligators, the skins of deer, panther, and wild-cat, are among his trophies. He asserted with vehemence that there were varieties of birds in Florida unknown as yet to any collection of natural history. He excited us greatly by speaking of a pair of pet pink curlews which had been tamed ; also of a snow-white stork, with sky-blue epaulet on each shoulder, which is to be found in the everglades. He was going to spend the whole summer alone in these regions, or only with Indian guides ; and seemed cheerful and enthusiastic. He should find plenty of cocoanuts, and would never need to have a fever if he would eat daily of the wild oranges which abound. If one only could go in spirit, and not in flesh, one would like to follow him into the everglades. The tropical forests of Florida contain visions and wonders of growth and glory never yet revealed to the eye of the common traveller, and which he who sees must risk much to explore. Our best wishes go with our enthusiast. May he live to tell us what he sees !

OUR NEIGHBOR OVER THE WAY.

OUR neighbor over the way is not, to be sure, quite so near or so observable as if one lived on Fifth Avenue or Broadway.

Between us and his cottage lie five good miles of molten silver in the shape of the St. John's River, outspread this morning in all its quivering sheen, glancing, dimpling, and sparkling, dotted with sail-boats, and occasionally ploughed by steamboats gliding like white swans back and forth across the distance.

Far over on the other side, where the wooded shores melt into pearly blue outlines, gleams out in the morning sun a white, glimmering spot about as big as a ninepence, which shows us where his cottage stands. Thither we are going to make a morning visit. Our water-coach is now approaching the little wharf front of our house : and we sally forth equipped with our sun-umbrellas ; for the middle of May here is like the middle of August at the North. The water-coach, or rather omnibus, is a little thimble of a steamer, built for pleasuring on the St. John's, called "The Mary Draper." She is a tiny shell of a thing, but with a nice, pretty cabin, and capable of carrying comfortably thirty or forty passengers. During the height of the travelling-season "The Mary Draper" is let out to

parties of tourists, who choose thus at their leisure
to explore the river, sailing, landing, rambling,
exploring, hunting, fishing, and perhaps inevi-
tably flirting among the flowery nooks and palmetto-hammocks of the shore. We have seen
her many a time coming gayly back from an excursion, with the voice of singing, and laugh of
youths and maidens, resounding from her deck,
flower-wreathed and flower-laden like some
fabled bark from the fairy isles. But now, in
the middle of May, the tourists are few ; and so
"The Mary Draper" has been turned into a sort
of errand-boat, plying up and down the river to
serve the needs and convenience of the permanent inhabitants. A flag shown upon our wharf
brings her in at our need ; and we step gayly on
board, to be carried across to our neighbors.

We take our seats at the shaded end of the
boat, and watch the retreating shore, with its
gigantic live-oaks rising like a dome above the

orange-orchards, its clouds of pink oleander-trees that seem every week to blossom fuller than the last; and for a little moment we can catch the snow-white glimmer of the great Cape jessamine-shrub that bends beneath the weight of flowers at the end of our veranda. Our little cottage looks like a rabbit's nest beside the monster oaks that shade it; but it is cosey to see them all out on the low veranda, — the Professor with his newspapers, the ladies with their worsteds and baskets, in fact the whole of our large family, — all reading, writing, working, in the shady covert of the orange-trees.

From time to time a handkerchief is waved on their part, and the signal returned on ours; and they follow our receding motions with a spy-glass. Our life is so still and lonely here, that even so small an event as our crossing the river for a visit is all-absorbing.

But, after a little, our craft melts off into the

distance, " The Mary Draper " looks to our friends
no larger than a hazel-nut, and the trees of the
other side loom up strong and tall in our eyes,
and grow clearer and clearer ; while our home,
with its great live-oaks and its orange-groves,
has all melted into a soft woolly haze of distance.
Our next neighbor's great whitewashed barn is
the only sign of habitation remaining ; and that
flashes out a mere shining speck in the distance.

Now the boat comes up to Mr. ——'s wharf ;
and he is there to meet and welcome us.

One essential to every country-house on the
St. John's is this accessory of a wharf and boat-
house. The river is, for a greater or less distance from the shore, too shallow to admit the
approach of steamboats ; and wharves of fifty
or a hundred feet in length are needed to enable
passengers to land.

The bottom of the river is of hard, sparkling
white sand, into which spiles are easily driven ;

and the building and keeping-up of such a wharf is a trifling trouble and expense in a land where lumber is so plentiful.

Our friend Mr. —— is, like many other old Floridian residents, originally from the North. In early youth he came to Florida a condemned and doomed consumptive, recovered his health, and has lived a long and happy life here, and acquired a handsome property.

He owns extensive tracts of rich and beautiful land on the west bank of the St. John's, between it and Jacksonville, destined, as that city grows and extends, to become of increasing value. His wife, like himself originally of Northern origin, has become perfectly acclimated and nat-uralized by years' residence at the South ; and is, to all intents and purposes, a Southern woman. They live all the year upon their place ; those who formerly were their slaves settled peaceably around them as free laborers, still looking up to them for advice, depending on them for aid, and rendering to them the willing, well-paid services of freemen.

Their house is a simple white cottage, situated so as to command a noble view of the river. A long avenue of young live-oak-trees leads up from the river to the house. The ground is covered with a smooth, even turf of Bermuda grass, — the only kind that will endure the burning glare of the tropical summer. The walls of the house are covered with roses, now in full bloom. La Marque, cloth-of-gold, and many another kind, throw out their splendid clusters, and fill the air with fragrance. We find Mrs. —— and her family on the veranda, — the usual reception-room in a Southern house. The house is the seat of hospitality; every room in it sure to be full, if not with the members of the family proper, then with guests from Jacksonville, who find, in this high, breezy situation, a charming retreat from the heat of the city.

One feature is characteristic of Southern houses, so far as we have seen. The ladies are enthusiastic plant-lovers ; and the veranda is lined round with an array of boxes in which gardening experiments are carried on. Rare plants, slips, choice seedlings, are here nurtured and cared for. In fact, the burning power of the tropical sun, and the scalding, fine white sand, is such, that to put a tender plant or slip into it seems, in the words of Scripture, like casting it into the oven ; and so there is everywhere more or less of this box-gardening.

The cottage was all in summer array ; the carpets taken up and packed away, leaving the smooth, yellow pine floors clean and cool as the French parquets.

The plan of the cottage is the very common one of Southern houses. A wide, clear hall, furnished as a sitting-room, opening on a veranda on either end, goes through the house ; and all the other rooms open upon it. We sat chatting, first on the veranda ; and, as the sun grew hotter, retreated inward to the hall, and discussed flowers, farm, and dairy.

On the east bank of the St. John's, where our own residence is, immediately around Mandarin, the pasturage is poor, and the cattle diminutive and half starved. Knowing that our neighbor was an old resident, and enthusiastic stock-raiser and breeder, we came to him for knowledge on these subjects. Stock-breeding has received a great share of attention from the larger planters of Florida. The small breed of wild native Florida cattle has been crossed and improved by foreign stock imported at great expense. The Brahmin cattle of India, as coming from a tropical region, were thought specially adapted to the Floridian climate, and have thriven well here. By crossing these with the Durham and Ayrshire and the native cattle, fine varieties of ani-

mals have been obtained.   Mr. —— showed me
a list of fifty of his finest cows, each one of which
has its distinguishing name, and with whose
pedigree and peculiarities he seemed well acquainted.

In rearing, the Floridian system has always
been to make every thing subservient to the increase of the herd.   The calf is allowed to run
with the cow; and the supply of milk for the
human being is only what is over and above the
wants of the calf.   The usual mode of milking is
to leave the calf sucking on one side, while the
milker sits on the other, and gets his portion.
It is an opinion fixed as fate in the mind of
every negro cow-tender, that to kill a calf would
be the death of the mother; and that, if you separate the calf from the mother, her milk will dry
up.   Fresh veal is a delicacy unheard of; and
once, when we suggested a veal-pie to a strapping
Ethiopian dairy-woman, she appeared as much

shocked as if we had proposed to fricassee a baby. Mr. ——, however, expressed his conviction that the Northern method of taking off the calf, and securing the cow's milk, could be practised with success, and had been in one or two cases. The yield of milk of some of the best blood cows was quite equal to that of Northern milkers, and might be kept up by good feeding. As a rule, however, stock-raisers depend for their supply of milk more on the number of their herd than the quantity given by each. The expenses of raising are not heavy where there is a wide expanse of good pasture-land for them to range in, and no necessity for shelters of any kind through the year.

Mr. —— spoke of the river-grass as being a real and valuable species of pasturage. On the west side of the river, the flats and shallows along by the shore are covered with a broad-leaved water-grass, very tender and nutritious, of which cattle are very fond.   It is a curious sight to see whole herds of cows browsing in the water, as one may do every day along the course of this river.

The subject of dairy-keeping came up ; and, at our request, Mrs. —— led the way to hers.   It is built out under a dense shade of trees in an airy situation, with double walls like an ice-house.   The sight of the snowy shelves set round with pans, on which a rich golden cream was forming, was a sufficient testimony that there could be beautiful, well-kept dairies in Florida, notwithstanding its tropical heats.

The butter is made every morning at an early hour ; and we had an opportunity of tasting it at the dinner-table.   Like the best butter of France and England, it is sweet and pure, like solidified cream, and as different as can be from the hard, salty mass which most generally passes for butter among us. The buttermilk of a daily churning is also sweet and rich, a delicious nourishing drink, and an excellent adjuvant in the making of various cakes and other household delicacies.

Our friend's experience satisfied us that there was no earthly reason in the climate or surroundings of Florida why milk and butter should be the scarce and expensive luxuries they are now. What one private gentleman can do simply for his own comfort and that of his family, we should think might be repeated on a larger scale by somebody in the neighborhood of Jacksonville as a money speculation. Along the western bank of this river are hundreds of tracts of good grazing land, where cattle might be pastured at small expense ; where the products of a dairy on a large scale would meet a ready and certain sale. At present the hotels and boarding-houses are supplied with condensed milk, and butter, imported from the North: and yet land is cheap here; labor is reasonable; the climate genial, requiring no outlay for shelter, and comparatively little necessity of storing food for winter. Fine breeds of animals of improved stock exist already, and can be indefinitely increased; and we wonder that nobody is to be found to improve the opportunity to run a stock and dairy farm which shall supply the hotels and boarding-houses of Jacksonville.

After visiting the dairy, we sauntered about, looking at the poultry-yards, where different breeds of hens, turkeys, pea-fowl, had each their allotted station. Four or five big dogs, hounds and pointers, trotted round with us, or rollicked with a party of grandchildren, assisted by the never-failing addition of a band of giggling little negroes. As in the old times, the servants of the family have their little houses back of the premises; and the laundry-work, &c., is carried on outside. The propensity at the South is to multiply little buildings. At the North, where there is a winter to be calculated on, the tactics of living are different. The effort is to gather all the needs and wants of life under one roof, to be warmed and kept in order at small expense. In the South, where building-material is cheap, and building is a slight matter, there is a separate little building for every thing; and the back part of an estate looks like an eruption of little houses. There is a milk-house, a corn-house, a tool-house, a bake-house, besides a house for each of the leading servants, making quite a village.

Our dinner was a bountiful display of the luxuries of a Southern farm, — finely-flavored fowl choicely cooked, fish from the river, 'soft-shell turtle-soup, with such a tempting variety of early vegetables as seemed to make it impossible to do justice to all. Mrs. —— offered us a fine sparkling wine made of the juice of the wild·

orange. In color it resembled the finest sherry, and was much like it in flavor.

We could not help thinking, as we refused dainty after dainty, from mere inability to take more, of the thoughtless way in which it is often said that there can be nothing fit to eat got in Florida.

Mr. ——'s family is supplied with food almost entirely from the products of his own farm. He has the nicest of fed beef, nice tender pork, poultry of all sorts, besides the resources of an ample, well-kept dairy. He raises and makes his own sirup. He has sweet-potatoes, corn, and all Northern vegetables, in perfection ; peaches, grapes of finest quality, besides the strictly tropical fruits ; and all that he has, any other farmer might also have with the same care.

After dinner we walked out to look at the grapes, which hung in profuse clusters, just beginning to ripen on the vines. On our way we stopped to admire a great bitter-sweet orange-tree, which seemed to make " Hesperian fables true." It was about thirty feet in height, and with branches that drooped to the ground, weighed down at the same time with great golden balls of fruit, and wreaths of pearly buds and blossoms. Every stage of fruit, from the tiny green ball of a month's growth to the perfected orange, were here ; all the processes of life going on together in joyous unity. The tree exemplified what an orange-tree could become when fully fed, when its almost boundless capacity for digesting nutriment meets a full supply ; and it certainly stood one of the most royal of trees. Its leaves were large, broad, and of that glossy, varnished green peculiar to the orange ; and its young shoots looked like burnished gold. The bitter-sweet orange is much prized by some. The pulp is sweet, with a certain spicy flavor ; but

16

the rind, and all the inner membranes that contain the fruit, are bitter as quinine itself. It is
held to be healthy to eat of both, as the acid
and the bitter are held to be alike correctives
of the bilious tendencies of the climate.

But the afternoon sun was casting the shadows the other way, and the little buzzing "Mary
Draper" was seen puffing in the distance on her
way back from Jacksonville ; and we walked
leisurely down the live-oak avenues to the wharf,
our hands full of roses and Oriental jessamine,
and many pleasant memories of our neighbors
over the way.

And now in relation to the general subject of
farming in Florida. Our own region east of the
St. John's River is properly a little sandy belt
of land, about eighteen miles wide, washed by
the Atlantic Ocean on one side, and the St.
John's River on the other. It is not by any
means so well adapted to stock-farming or

general farming as the western side of the river. Its principal value is in fruit-farming ; and it will appear, by a voyage up the river, that all the finest old orange-groves and all the new orange-plantations are on the eastern side of the river.

The presence, on either side, of two great bodies of water, produces a more moist and equable climate, and less liability to frosts. In the great freeze of 1835, the orange-groves of the west bank were killed beyond recovery ; while the fine groves of Mandarin sprang up again from the root, and have been vigorous bearers for years since.

But opposite Mandarin, along the western shore, lie miles and miles of splendid land — which in the olden time produced cotton of the finest quality, sugar, rice, sweet-potatoes — now growing back into forest with a tropical rapidity. The land lies high, and affords fine sites for dwellings ; and the region is comparatively healthy.

Then Hibernia, Magnolia, and Green Cove, on the one side, and Jacksonville on the other, show perfect assemblages of boarding-houses and hotels, where ready market might be found for what good farmers might raise. A colony of farmers coming out and settling here together, bringing with them church and schoolhouse, with a minister skilled like St. Bernard both in husbandry and divinity, might soon create a thrifty farming-village. We will close this chapter with an extract from a letter of a Northern emigrant recently settled at Newport, on the north part of Appalachicola Bay.

SEPT. 22, 1872.

I have been haying this month: in fact I had mowed my orange-grove, a square of two acres, from time to time, all summer. But this month a field of two acres had a heavy burden of grass, with cow-pease intermixed. In some parts of the field, there certainly would be at the rate of three tons to the acre. The whole field would average one ton to the acre. So I went at it with a good Northern scythe, and mowed every morning an hour or two. The hay was perfectly cured by five, P.M., same day, and put in barn. The land, being in ridges, made mowing difficult. Next year I mean to lay that land down to grass, taking out stumps, and making smooth, sowing rye and clover. I shall plough it now as soon as the hay is all made, and sow the rye and clover immediately. I have five cows that give milk, and four that should come in soon. These, with their calves, I shall feed through the months when the grass is poor. I have also a yoke of oxen and four young steers, with Trim the mule. I have already in the barn three to four tons of hay and corn-fodder, and two acres of cow-pease cured, to be used as hay. I hope to have five hundred bushels of sweet-potatoes, which, for stock, are equal to corn. I made a hundred and ten bushels of corn, twenty-five to the acre. My cane is doing moderately well. Hope to have all the seed I want to plant fourteen acres next year. Bananas thrive beautifully; shall have fifty offsets to set out this winter; also three or four thousand oranges, all large-sized and fair.

All these facts go to show, that; while Florida cannot compete with the Northern and Western States as a grass-raising State, yet there are other advantages in her climate and productions which make stock-farming feasible and profitable. The disadvantages of her burning climate may, to a degree, be evaded and overcome by the application of the same patient industry and ingenuity which rendered fruitful the iron soil and freezing climate of the New-England States.

THE GRAND TOUR UP RIVER.

THE St. John's is the grand water-highway through some of the most beautiful portions of Florida ; and tourists, safely seated at ease on the decks of steamers, can penetrate into the mysteries and wonders of unbroken tropical forests.

During the "season," boats continually run from Jacksonville to Enterprise, and back again ; the round trip being made for a moderate sum, and giving, in a very easy and comparatively inexpensive manner, as much of the peculiar scenery as mere tourists care to see. On returning, a digression is often made at Tekoi, where passengers cross a horse-railroad of fifteen miles to St. Augustine; thus rendering their survey of East Florida more complete. In fact, what may be seen and known of the State in such a trip is about all that the majority of tourists see and know.

The great majority also perform this trip, and see this region, in the dead of winter, when certainly one-half of the glorious forests upon the shore are bare of leaves.

It is true that the great number of evergreen-trees here make the shores at all times quite different from those of a Northern climate; yet the difference between spring and winter is as great here as there.

Our party were resolute in declining all invitations to join parties in January, February, and March; being determined to wait till the new spring foliage was in its glory.

When the magnolia-flowers were beginning to blossom, we were ready, and took passage — a joyous party of eight or ten individuals — on the steamer " Darlington," commanded by Capt. Broch, and, as is often asserted, by " Commodore Rose."

This latter, in this day of woman's rights, is no mean example of female energy and vigor. She is stewardess of the boat, and magnifies her office. She is a colored woman, once a slave owned by Capt. Broch, but emancipated, as the story goes, for her courage, and presence of mind, in saving his life in a steamboat disaster.

Rose is short and thick, weighing some two or three hundred, with a brown complexion, and a pleasing face and fine eyes. Her voice, like that of most colored women, is soft, and her manner

of speaking pleasing.   All this, however, relates
to her demeanor when making the agreeable to
passengers.   In other circumstances, doubtless,
she can speak louder, and with considerable more
emphasis ; and show, in short, those martial attri-
butes which have won for her the appellation of
the "Commodore."   It is asserted that the whole
charge of provisioning and running the boat, and
all its internal arrangements, vests in Madam
Rose ; and that nobody can get ahead of her in
a bargain, or resist her will in an arrangement.

She knows every inch of the river, every house,
every plantation along shore, its former or
present occupants and history ; and is always
ready with an answer to a question.   The
arrangement and keeping of the boat do honor
to her.   Nowhere in Florida does the guest sit
at a more bountifully-furnished table.   Our
desserts and pastry were really, for the wilder-
ness, something quite astonishing.

The St. John's River below Pilatka has few distinguishing features to mark it out from other great rivers. It is so wide, that the foliage of the shores cannot be definitely made out ; and the tourist here, expecting his palm-trees and his magnolias and flowering-vines, is disappointed by sailing in what seems a never-ending great lake, where the shores are off in the distance too far to make out any thing in particular. But, after leaving Pilatka, the river grows narrower, the overhanging banks approach nearer, and the foliage becomes more decidedly tropical in its character. Our boat, after touching as usual at Hibernia, Magnolia, and Green Cove, brought up at Pilatka late in the afternoon, made but a short stop, and was on her way again.

It was the first part of May ; and the forests were in that fulness of leafy perfection which they attain in the month of June at the North. But there is a peculiar, vivid brilliancy about the green of the new spring-leaves here, which we never saw elsewhere. It is a brilliancy like some of the new French greens, now so much in vogue, and reminding one of the metallic brightness of birds and insects. In the woods, the cypress is a singular and beautiful feature. It attains to a great age and immense size. The trunk and branches of an old cypress are smooth and white as ivory, while its light, feathery foliage is of the most dazzling golden-green ; and rising, as it often does, amid clumps of dark varnished evergreens, — bay and magnolia and myrtle, — it has a singular and beautiful effect. The long swaying draperies of the gray moss interpose everywhere their wavering outlines and pearl tints amid the brightness and bloom of the forest, giving to its deep recesses the mystery of grottoes hung with fanciful vegetable stalactites.

The palmetto-tree appears in all stages, — from

its earliest growth, when it looks like a fountain of great, green fan-leaves bursting from the earth, to its perfect shape, when, sixty or seventy feet in height, it rears its fan crown high in air. The oldest trees may be known by a perfectly smooth trunk ; all traces of the scaly formation by which it has built itself up in ring after ring of leaves being obliterated. But younger trees, thirty or forty feet in height, often show a trunk which seems to present a regular criss-cross of basket-work, — the remaining scales from whence the old leaves have decayed and dropped away. These scaly trunks are often full of ferns, wild flowers, and vines, which hang in fantastic draperies down their sides, and form leafy and flowery pillars. The palmetto-hammocks, as they are called, are often miles in extent along the banks of the rivers. The tops of the palms rise up round in the distance as so many hay-cocks, and seeming to rise one above another far as the eye can reach.

We have never been so fortunate as to be able to explore one of these palmetto-groves. The boat sails with a provoking quickness by many a scene that one longs to dwell upon, study, and investigate. We have been told, however, by hunters, that they afford admirable camping-ground, being generally high and dry, with a flooring of clean white sand. Their broad leaves are a perfect protection from rain and dew ; and the effect of the glare of the camp-fires and torch-lights on the tall pillars, and waving, fan-like canopy overhead, is said to be perfectly magical. The most unromantic and least impressible speak of it with enthusiasm.

In going up the river, darkness overtook us shortly after leaving Pilatka. We sat in a golden twilight, and saw the shores every moment becoming more beautiful ; but when the twilight faded, and there was no moon, we sought the repose of our cabin. It was sultry as August, although only the first part of May ; and our younger and sprightlier members, who were on the less breezy side of the boat, after fruitlessly trying to sleep, arose and dressed themselves, and sat all night on deck.

By this means they saw a sight worth seeing, and one which we should have watched all night to see. The boat's course at night is through narrows of the river, where we could hear the crashing and crackling of bushes and trees, and sometimes a violent thud, as the boat, in turning a winding, struck against the bank. On the forward part two great braziers were kept filled with blazing, resinous light-wood, to guide the pilot in the path of the boat. The effect of this glare of red light as the steamer passed through the palmetto hummocks and moss-hung grottoes of the forest was something that must have been indescribably weird and beautiful ; and our young friends made us suitably regret that our more airy sleeping-accommodations had lost us this experience.

In the morning we woke at Enterprise, having come through all the most beautiful and characteristic part of the way by night. Enterprise is some hundred and thirty miles south of our dwelling-place in Mandarin; and, of course, that much nearer the tropical regions. We had planned excursions, explorations, picnics in the woods, and a visit to the beautiful spring in the neighborhood; but learned with chagrin that the boat made so short a stay, that none of these things were possible. The only thing that appears to the naked eye of a steamboat traveller in Enterprise is a large hotel down upon the landing, said by those who have tested it to be one of the best kept hotels in Florida. The aspect of the shore just there is no way picturesque or inviting, but has more that forlorn, ragged, desolate air that new settlements on the river are apt to have. The wild, untouched banks are beautiful ; but the new settlements generally succeed in destroying all Nature's beauty, and give you only leafless, girdled trees, blackened stumps, and naked white sand, in return.

Turning our boat homeward, we sailed in clear morning light back through the charming scenery which we had slept through the night before. It is the most wild, dream-like, enchanting sail conceivable. The river sometimes narrows so that the boat brushes under overhanging branches, and then widens into beautiful lakes dotted with wooded islands. Palmetto-hammocks, live-oak groves, cypress, pine, bay, and magnolia form an interchanging picture ; vines hang festooned from tree to tree ; wild flowers tempt the eye on the near banks ; and one is constantly longing for the boat to delay here or there : but on goes her steady course, the pictured scene

17

around constantly changing. Every now and then the woods break away for a little space, and one sees orange and banana orchards, and houses evidently newly built. At many points the boat landed, and put off kegs of nails, hoes, ploughs, provisions, groceries. Some few old plantations were passed, whose name and history seemed familiar to Madam Rose ; but by far the greater number were new settlements, with orchards of quite young trees, which will require three or four more years to bring into bearing.

The greater number of fruit-orchards and settlements were on the eastern shore of the river, which, for the reasons we have spoken of, is better adapted to the culture of fruit.

One annoyance on board the boat was the constant and pertinacious firing kept up by that class of men who think that the chief end of man is to shoot something. Now, we can put up with good earnest hunting or fishing done for the purpose of procuring for man food, or even the fur and feathers that hit his fancy and taste.

But we detest indiscriminate and purposeless maiming and killing of happy animals, who have but one life to live, and for whom the agony of broken bones or torn flesh is a helpless, hopeless pain, unrelieved by any of the resources which enable us to endure. A parcel of hulking fellows sit on the deck of a boat, and pass through the sweetest paradise God ever made, without one idea of its loveliness, one gentle, sympathizing thought of the animal happiness with which the Creator has filled these recesses. All the way along is a constant fusillade upon every living thing that shows itself on the bank. Now a bird is hit, and hangs, head downward, with a broken wing; and a coarse laugh choruses the deed. Now an alligator is struck; and the applause is greater. We once saw a harmless young alligator, whose dying struggles, as he threw out his poor little black paws piteously like human hands, seemed to be vastly diverting to these cultivated individuals. They wanted nothing of him except to see how he would act when he was hit, dying agonies are so very amusing!

Now and then these sons of Nimrod in their zeal put in peril the nerves, if not lives, of passengers. One such actually fired at an alligator right across a crowd of ladies, many of them invalids; and persisted in so firing a second time, after having been requested to desist. If the object were merely to show the skill of the marksman, why not practise upon inanimate objects? An old log looks much like an alligator: why not practise on an old log? It requires as much skill to hit a branch, as the bird singing on it: why not practise on the branch? But no: it must be something that *enjoys* and can suffer; something that loves life, and must lose it. Certainly this in an inherent savagery difficult to account for. Killing for killing's sake belongs not even to the tiger. The tiger kills for food ; man, for amusement.

At evening we were again at Pilatka ; when the great question was discussed, Would we, or would we not, take the tour up the Okalewaha to see the enchanted wonders of the Silver Spring! The Okalewaha boat lay at the landing ; and we went to look at it. The Okalewaha is a deep, narrow stream, by the by, emptying into the St. John's, with a course as crooked as Apollo's ram's horn ; and a boat has been constructed for the express purpose of this passage.

The aspect of this same boat on a hot night was not inspiriting. It was low, long, and narrow ; its sides were rubbed glassy smooth, or torn and creased by the friction of the bushes and trees it had pushed through. It was without glass windows, — which would be of no use in such navigation, — and, in place thereof, furnished with strong shutters to close the air-holes.   We looked at this same thing as it lay like a gigantic coffin in the twilight, and thought even the Silver Spring would not pay for being immured there, and turned away.

A more inviting project was to step into a sail-boat, and be taken in the golden twilight over to Col. Harte's orange-grove, which is said — with reason, we believe — to be the finest in Florida.

We landed in the twilight in this grove of six hundred beautiful orange-trees in as high condition as the best culture could make them.   The well-fed orange-tree is known by the glossy, deep green of its foliage, as a declining tree is by the yellow tinge of its leaves.   These trees looked as if each leaf, if broken, would spurt with juice. Piles of fish-guano and shell banks, prepared as top-dress for the orchard, were lying everywhere about, mingling not agreeably with the odor of orange-blossoms. We thought to ourselves, that, if the orange-orchard must be fed upon putrefying fish, we should prefer not to have a house in it. The employee who has charge of the orchard lives in a densely-shaded cottage in the edge of it. A large fruit-house has recently been built there ; and the experiments of Col. Harte seem to demonstrate, that, even if there occur severe frosts in the early winter, there is no sort of need, therefore, of losing the orange-crop. His agent showed us oranges round and fair that had been kept three months in moss in this fruit-house, and looking as fresh and glossy as those upon the trees. This, if proved by experience, always possible, does away with the only uncertainty relating to the orange-crop. Undoubtedly the fruit is far better to continue all winter on the trees, and be gathered from time to time as wanted, as has always been the practice in Florida. But, with fruit-houses and moss, it will be possible, in case of a threatened fall of temperature, to secure the crop. The oranges that come to us from Malaga and Sicily are green as grass when gathered and packed, and ripen, as much as they do ripen, on the voyage over. We should suppose the oranges of Florida might be gathered much nearer ripe in the fall, ripen in the house or on the way, and still be far better than any from the foreign market. On this point fruit-growers are now instituting experiments, which, we trust, will make this delicious crop certain as it is abundant.

Sailing back across the water, we landed, and were conveyed to the winter country-seat of a Brooklyn gentleman, who is with great enthusiasm cultivating a place there. It was almost dark ; and we could only hear of his gardens and grounds and improvements, not see them. In the morning, before the boat left the landing, he took us a hasty drive around the streets of the little village. It is an unusually pretty, attractive - looking place for a Florida settlement. One reason for this is, that the streets and vacant lots are covered with a fine green turf, which, at a distance, looks like our New-England grass. It is a mixture of Bermuda grass with a variety of herbage, and has just as good general effect as if it were the best red-top.

There are several fine residences in and around Pilatka, — mostly winter-seats of Northern settlers. The town has eight stores, which do a business for all the surrounding country for miles. It has two large hotels, several boarding-houses, two churches, two steam saw-mills, and is the headquarters for the steamboats of the Upper St. John's and its tributaries. Four or five steamers from different quarters are often stopping at its wharf at a time. "The Dictator" and "City Point," from Charleston, run to this place outside by the ocean passage, and, entering the mouth of the St. John's, stop at Jacksonville by the way. The "Nick King" and "Lizzie Baker," in like manner, make what is called the inside trip, skimming through the network of islands that line the coast, and bringing up at the same points. Then there are the river-lines continually plying between Jacksonville and this place, and the small boats that run weekly to the Ocklawaha: all these make Pilatka a busy, lively, and important place.

With Pilatka the interest of our return-voyage finished. With Green-Cove Spring, Magnolia, Hibernia, at all of which we touched on our way back, we were already familiar; and the best sight of all was the cottage under the oaks, to which we gladly returned.

OLD CUDJO AND THE ANGEL.

THE little wharf at Mandarin is a tiny abutment into the great blue sea of the St. John's waters, five miles in width. The opposite shores gleam out blue in the vanishing distance ; and the small wharf is built so far out, that one feels there as in a boat at sea. Here, trundled down on the truck along a descending tram-way, come the goods which at this point await shipment on some of the many steamboats which ply back and forth upon the river ; and here are landed by almost every steamer goods and chattels for the many families which are hidden in the shaddows of the forests that clothe the river's shore. In sight are scarce a dozen houses, all told ; but far back, for a radius of ten or fifteen miles, are scattered farmhouses whence come tributes of produce to this point. Hundreds of barrels of oranges, boxes of tomatoes and early vegetables, grapes, peaches, and pomegranates, here pause on their way to the Jacksonville market.

One morning, as the Professor and I were enjoying our morning stroll on the little wharf, an unusual sight met our eye, — a bale of cotton, long and large, pressed hard and solid as iron, and done up and sewed in a wholly workmanlike manner, that excited our surprise. It was the first time since we had been in Mandarin — a space of some four or five years — that we had

ever seen a bale of cotton on that wharf. Yet
the whole soil of East Florida is especially
adapted not only to the raising of cotton, but of
the peculiar, long staple cotton which commands
the very highest market-price. But for two or
three years past the annual ravages of the cotton-worm had been so discouraging, that the culture of cotton had been abandoned in despair.

Whence, then, had come that most artistic
bale of cotton, so well pressed, so trim and tidy,
and got up altogether in so superior a style ?

Standing by it on the wharf was an aged
negro, misshapen, and almost deformed. He was
thin and bony, and his head and beard were griz-
zled with age. He was black as night itself;
and but for a glittering, intellectual eye, he
might have been taken for a big baboon, — the
missing link of Darwin. To him spoke the Professor, giving a punch with his cane upon the
well-packed, solid bale : —

" Why, this is splendid cotton ! Where did it come from ? Who raised it ? "

"*We* raise it, sah, — me 'n' dis yer boy," pointing to a middle-aged black man beside him : " we raise it."

" Where ? "

" Oh ! out he'yr a piece."

A lounging white man, never wanting on a wharf, here interposed : —

" Oh ! this is old Cudjo. He lives up Julington. He's an honest old fellow."

Now, we had heard of this settlement up Julington some two or three years before. A party of negroes from South Carolina and Georgia had been induced to come into Florida, and take up a tract of government land. Some white man in whom they all put confidence had undertaken for them the task of getting their respective allotments surveyed and entered for them, so that they should have a solid basis of land to work upon.

Here, then, they settled down ; and finding, acci-
dentally, that a small central lot was not enclosed
in any of the allotments, they took it as an indica-
tion that *there* was to be their church, and accordingly erected there a prayer-booth, where they
could hold those weekly prayer-meetings which
often seem with the negroes to take the place of
all other recreations. The neighboring farmers
were not particularly well disposed towards the
little colony. The native Floridian farmer is a
quiet, peaceable being, not at all disposed to in-
fringe the rights of others, and mainly anxious for
peace and quietness. But they supposed that a
stampede of negroes from Georgia and Carolina
meant trouble for them, meant depredations upon
their cattle and poultry, and regarded it with no
friendly eye ; yet, nevertheless, they made no
demonstration against it. Under these circumstances, the new colony had gone to work with untiring industry. They had built log-cabins and

barns ; they had split rails, and fenced in their land ; they had planted orange-trees ; they had cleared acres of the scrub-palmetto : and any one that ever has seen what it is to clear up an acre of scrub-palmetto will best appreciate the meaning of that toil. Only those black men, with sinews of steel and nerves of wire, — men who grow stronger and more vigorous under those burning suns that wither the white men, — are competent to the task.

But old Cudjo had at last brought his land from the wild embrace of the snaky scrub-palmetto to the point of bearing a bale of cotton like the one on the wharf. He had subdued the savage earth, brought her under, and made her tributary to his will, and demonstrated what the soil of East Florida might, could, and would do, the cotton-worm to the contrary notwithstanding.

And yet this morning he stood by his cotton, drooping and dispossessed. The white man that had engaged to take up land for these colonists had done his work in such a slovenly, imperfect manner, that another settler, a foreigner, had taken up a tract which passed right through old Cudjo's farm, and taken the land on which he had spent four years of hard work, — taken his log-cabin and barn and young trees, and the very piece that he had just brought to bearing that bale of cotton. And there he stood by it, mournful and patient. It was only a continuation of what he had always experienced, — always oppressed, always robbed and cheated. Old Cudjo was making the best of it in trying to ship his bale of cotton, which was all that was left of four years' toil.

"What!" said the Professor to him, "are you the old man that has been turned out by that foreigner?"

"Yes, sah!" he said, his little black eyes kindling, and quivering from head to foot with ex-

citement. "He take ebry t'ing, ebry t'ing,—
my house I built myself, my fences, and more'n
t'ree t'ousand rails I split myself : he take 'em
all !"

There is always some bitter spot in a great loss
that is sorer than the rest. Those rails evidently
cut Cudjo to the heart. The "t'ree t'ousand
rails" kept coming in in his narrative as the utter
and unbearable aggravation of injustice.

"I split 'em myself, sah ; *ebry one*, t'ree t'ousand rails ! and he take 'em all !"

"And won't he allow you any thing ?"

"No, sah : he won't 'low me not'ing. He say,
'Get along wid you ! don't know not'ing 'bout
you ! dis yer land mine.' I tell him, '*You* don't
know old Cudjo ; but de Lord know him : and
by'm by, when de angel Gabriel come and put
one foot on de sea, and t'odder on de land, and
blow de trumpet, he blow once for old Cudjo !
You mind now !'"

This was not merely spoken, but acted. The old black kindled, and stepped off in pantomime. He put, as it were, one foot on the sea, and the other on the land ; he raised his cane trumpet-wise to his mouth. It was all as vivid as reality to him.

None of the images of the Bible are more frequent, favorite, and operative among the black race than this. You hear it over and over in every prayer-meeting. It is sung in wild chorus in many a "spiritual." The great angel Gabriel, the trumpet, the mighty pomp of a last judgment, has been the appeal of thousands of wronged, crushed, despairing hearts through ages of oppression. Faith in God's justice, faith in a final triumph of right over wrong, — a practical faith, — such had been the attainment of this poor, old, deformed black. That and his bale of cotton were all he had to show for a life's labor. He had learned two things in his world-lesson, — work and

faith.   He had learned the power of practical industry in things possible to man : he had learned
the sublimer power of faith in God for things impossible.

.   .   .   .

Well, of course we were indignant enough about
poor old Cudjo : but we feared that the distant
appeal of the angel, and the last trump, was all
that remained to him ; and, to our lesser faith,
that seemed a long way to look for justice.

But redress was nearer than we imagined.   Old
Cudjo's patient industry and honest work had
wrought favor among his white neighbors.   He
had lived down the prejudice with which the settlement had first been regarded ; for among quiet,
honest people like the Floridians, it is quite possible to live down prejudice.   A neighboring justice
of the peace happened to have an acquaintance in
Washington from this very district, acquainted
with all the land and land-titles.   He wrote to this

man an account of the case ; and he interested himself for old Cudjo. He went to the land-office to investigate the matter. He found, that, in both cases, certain formalities necessary to constitute a legal entrance had been omitted ; and he fulfilled for old Cudjo these formalities, thus settling his title ; and, moreover, he sent legal papers by which the sheriff of the county was enabled to do him justice : and so old Cudjo was re-instated in his rights.

The Professor met him, sparkling and jubilant, on the wharf once more.

" Well, Cudjo, ' de angel ' blew for you quicker than you expected."

He laughed all over. " Ye', haw, haw ! Yes, massa." Then, with his usual histrionic vigor, he acted over the scene. " De sheriff, he come down dere. He tell dat man, ' You go right off he'yr. Don't you touch none dem rails. Don't you take one chip, — not one chip. Don't you take ' — Haw, haw, haw ! " Then he added, —

"He come to me, sah : he say, 'Cudjo, what you take for your land ?' He say he gib me two hunder dollars. I tell him, 'Dat too cheap; dat all too cheap.' He say, 'Cudjo, what will you take ?' I say, 'I take ten t'ousand million dollars ! dat's what I take.' Haw, haw, haw!"

THE LABORERS OF THE SOUTH.

WHO shall do the work for us? is the inquiry in this new State, where there are marshes to be drained, forests to be cut down, palmetto-plains to be grubbed up, and all under the torrid heats of a tropical sun.

"Chinese," say some; "Swedes," say others; "Germans," others.

But let us look at the facts before our face and eyes.

The thermometer, for these three days past, has risen over ninety every day. No white man that we know of dares stay in the fields later than ten o'clock: then he retires under shade to take some other and less-exposing work. The fine white sand is blistering hot: one might fancy that an egg would cook, as on Mt. Vesuvius, by simply burying it in the sand. Yet the black laborers whom we leave in the field pursue their toil, if any thing, more actively, more cheerfully, than during the cooler months. The sun awakes all their vigor and all their boundless jollity. When their nooning time comes, they sit down, not in the shade, but in some good hot place in the sand, and eat their lunch, and then stretch out, hot and comfortable, to take their noon siesta with the full glare of the sun upon them. Down in the swamp-land near our house we have watched old Simon as from hour to hour he drove his wheelbarrow, heavy with blocks of muck, up a steep bank, and deposited it. " Why, Simon !" we say : " how *can* you work so this hot weather ? "

The question provokes an explosion of laughter. " Yah, hah, ho, ho, ho, misse ! It be hot ; dat so : ho, ho, ho ! "

" How *can* you work so ? I can't even think how you can do such hard work under such a sun."

" Dat so : ho, ho ! Ladies can't ; no, dey can't, bless you, ma'am ! " And Simon trundles off with his barrow, chuckling in his might ; comes up with another load, throws it down, and chuckles again. A little laugh goes a great way with Simon ; for a boiling spring of animal content is ever welling up within.

One tremendously hot day, we remember our steamer stopping at Fernandina. Owing to the state of the tide, the wharf was eight or ten feet above the boat ; and the plank made a steep in-

clined plane, down which a mountain of multi
farious freight was to be shipped on our boat.
A gang of negroes, great, brawny, muscular fellows, seemed to make a perfect frolic of this job,
which, under such a sun, would have threatened
sunstroke to any white man. How they ran and
shouted and jabbered, and sweated their shirts
through, as one after another received on their
shoulders great bags of cotton-seed, or boxes
and bales, and ran down the steep plane with
them into the boat! At last a low, squat giant
of a fellow, with the limbs and muscles of a great
dray-horse, placed himself in front of a large
truck, and made his fellows pile it high with
cotton-bags; then, holding back with a prodi-
gious force, he took the load steadily down the
steep plane till within a little of the bottom,
when he dashed suddenly forward, and landed
it half across the boat. This feat of gigantic
strength he repeated again and again, running up

each time apparently as fresh as if nothing had happened, shouting, laughing, drinking quarts of water, and sweating like a river-god. Never was harder work done in a more jolly spirit.

Now, when one sees such sights as these, one may be pardoned for thinking that the negro is the natural laborer of tropical regions. He is immensely strong; he thrives and flourishes physically under a temperature that exposes a white man to disease and death.

The malarial fevers that bear so hard on the white race have far less effect on the negro: it is rare that they have what are called here the "shakes;" and they increase and multiply, and bear healthy children, in situations where the white race deteriorate and grow sickly.

On this point we had an interesting conversation with a captain employed in the Government Coast Survey. The duties of this survey involve much hard labor, exposure to the fiercest extremes of tropical temperature, and sojourning and travelling in swamps and lagoons, often most deadly to the white race. For this reason, he manned his vessel with a crew composed entirely of negroes ; and he informed us that the result had been perfectly satisfactory. The negro constitution enabled them to undergo with less suffering and danger the severe exposure and toils of the enterprise ; and the gayety and good nature which belonged to the race made their toils seem to sit lighter upon them than upon a given number of white men. He had known them, after a day of heavy exposure, travelling through mud and swamps, and cutting saw-grass, which wounds like a knife, to sit down at evening, and sing songs and play on the banjo, laugh and tell stories, in the very best of spirits. He furthermore valued them for their docility, and perfect subjection to discipline.

He announced strict rules, forbidding all drunkenness and profanity ; and he never found a difficulty in enforcing these rules : their obedience and submission were perfect. When this gentleman was laid up with an attack of fever in St. Augustine, his room was beset by anxious negro mammies, relations of his men, bringing fruits, flowers, and delicacies of their compounding for " the captain."

Those who understand and know how to treat the negroes seldom have reason to complain of their ingratitude.

But it is said, by Northern men who come down with Northern habits of labor, that the negro is inefficient as a laborer.

It is to be conceded that the influence of climate and constitution, and the past benumbing influences of slavery, do make the habits of Southern laborers very different from the habits of Northern men, accustomed, by the shortness of summer and the length of winter, to set the utmost value on their working-time.

In the South, where growth goes on all the year round, there really is no need of that intense, driving energy and vigilance in the use of time that are needed in the short summers of the North : an equal amount can be done with less labor.

But the Northern man when he first arrives, before he has proved the climate, looks with impatient scorn on what seems to him the slow, shilly-shally style in which both black and white move on. It takes an attack of malarial fever or two to teach him that he cannot labor the day through under a tropical sun as he can in the mountains of New Hampshire. After a shake or two of this kind, he comes to be thankful if he can hire Cudjo or Pompey to plough and hoe in his fields through the blazing hours, even though they do not plough and hoe with all the alacrity of Northern farmers.

It is also well understood, that, in taking negro laborers, we have to take men and women who have been educated under a system the very worst possible for making good, efficient, careful, or honest laborers. Take any set of white men, and put them for two or three generations under the same system of work without wages, forbid them legal marriage and secure family ties, and we will venture to predict that they would come out of the ordeal a much worse set than the Southern laborers are.

We have had in our own personal experience pretty large opportunities of observation. Immediately after the war, two young New-England men hired the Mackintosh Plantation, opposite to Mandarin, on the west bank of the St. John's River. It was, in old times, the model plantation of Florida, employing seven hundred negroes, raising sugar, rice, Sea-Island cotton. There was upon it a whole village of well-built, comfortable negro houses, — as well built and comfortable as those of any of the white small farmers around. There was a planter's house ; a schoolhouse, with chambers for the accommodation of a teacher, who was to instruct the planter's children. There were barns, and a cotton-gin and storehouse, a sugar-house, a milk and dairy house, an oven, and a kitchen ; each separate buildings. There were some two or three hundred acres of cleared land, fit for the raising of cotton. This whole estate had been hired by these young men on the principle of sharing half the profits with the owner. After they had carried it on one year, some near relatives became partners ; and then we were frequent visitors there. About thirty laboring families were employed upon the place. These were from different, more northern States, who had drifted downward after the Emancipation Act to try the new luxury of being free to choose their own situation, and seek their own fortune. Some were from Georgia, some from South and some from North Carolina, and some from New Orleans ; in fact, the *débris* of slavery, washed together in the tide of emancipation. Such as they were, they were a fair specimen of the Southern negro as slavery had made and left him.

The system pursued with them was not either patronizing or sentimental. The object was to put them at once on the ground of free white men and women, and to make their labor profitable to their employers. They were taught the nature of a contract ; and their agreements with their employers were all drawn up in writing, and explained to them. The terms were a certain monthly sum of money, rations for the month, rent of cottage, and privileges of milk from the dairy. One of the most efficient and intelligent was appointed to be foreman of the plantation ; and he performed the work of old

performed by a driver.   He divided the hands
into gangs ; appointed their places in the field ;
settled any difficulties between them ; and, in fact,
was an overseer of the detail.   Like all unedu-
cated people, the negroes are great conservatives.
They clung to the old ways of working, — to the
gang, the driver, and the old field arrangements,
— even where one would have thought another
course easier and wiser.

In the dim gray of the morning, Mose blew
his horn ; and all turned out and worked their
two or three hours without breakfast, and then
came back to their cabins to have corn-cake
made, and pork fried, and breakfast prepared.
We suggested that the New-England manner
of an early breakfast would be more to the purpose ; but were met by the difficulty, nay, almost
impossibility, of making the negroes work in
any but the routine to which they had been
accustomed.   But in this routine they worked

honestly, cheerfully, and with a will. They had the fruits of their labors constantly in hand, in the form either of rations or wages ; and there appeared to be much sober content therewith.

On inquiry, it was found, that, though living in all respectability in families, the parties were, many of them, not legally married ; and an attempt was made to induce them to enter into holy orders. But the men seemed to regard this as the imposing of a yoke beyond what they could bear. Mose said he had one wife in Virginny, and one in Carliny ; and how did he know which of 'em he should like best ? Mandy, on the female side, objected that she could not be married yet for want of a white lace veil, which she seemed to consider essential to the ceremony. The survey of Mandy in her stuff gown and cow-hide boots, with her man's hat on, following the mule with the plough, brought rather ludicrous emotions in connection with this want of a white veil.

Nevertheless, the legal marriages were few among them. They lived faithfully in their respective family relations ; and they did their work, on the whole, effectively and cheerfully. Their only amusement, after working all day, seemed to be getting together, and holding singing and prayer meetings, which they often did to a late hour of the night. We used to sit and hear them, after ten or eleven o'clock, singing and praying and exhorting with the greatest apparent fervor. There were one or two of what are called preachers among them, — men with a natural talent for stringing words together, and with fine voices. As a matter of curiosity, we once sat outside, when one of these meetings was going on, to hear what it was like.

The exhortation seemed to consist in a string of solemn-sounding words and phrases, images borrowed from Scripture, scraps of hymns, and now and then a morsel that seemed like a

Roman-Catholic tradition about the Virgin Mary and Jesus. The most prominent image, however, was that of the angel, and the blowing of the last trumpet. At intervals, amid the flying cloud of images and words, came round something about Gabriel and the last trump, somewhat as follows : " And He will say, ' Gabriel, Gabriel, blow your trump : take it cool and easy, cool and easy, Gabriel : dey's all bound for to come.' "

This idea of taking even the blowing of the last trump cool and easy seemed to be so like the general negro style of attending to things, that it struck me as quite refreshing. As to singing, the most doleful words with the most lugubrious melodies seemed to be in favor.

" Hark ! from the tombs a doleful sound,"

was a special favorite. With eyes shut, and mouth open, they would pour out a perfect storm of minor-keyed melody on poor old Dr. Watts's hymn, mispronouncing every word, till the old doctor himself could not have told whether they were singing English or Timbuctoo.

Yet all this was done with a fervor and earnest solemnity that seemed to show that *they* found something in it, whether we could or not: who shall say? A good old mammy we used to know found great refreshment in a hymn, the chorus of which was, —

> "Bust the bonds of dust and thunder;
> Bring salvation from on high."

Undoubtedly the words suggested to her very different ideas from what they did to us; for she obstinately refused to have them exchanged for good English. But when the enlightened, wise, liberal, and refined for generations have found edification and spiritual profit from a service chanted in an unknown tongue, who shall say that the poor negroes of our plantation did not derive real spiritual benefit from their night services? It was at least an aspiration, a reaching and longing for something above animal and physical good, a recognition of God and immortality, and a future beyond this earth, vague and indefinite though it were.

As to the women, they were all of the class born and bred as field-hands. They were many of them as strong as men, could plough and chop and cleave with the best, and were held to be among the best field-laborers; but, in all household affairs, they were as rough and unskilled as might be expected. To mix meal, water, and salt into a hoe-cake, and to fry salt pork or ham or chicken, was the extent of their knowledge of cooking; and as to sewing, it is a fortunate thing that the mild climate requires very slight covering. All of them practised, rudely, cutting, fitting, and making of garments to cover their children ; but we could see how hard was their task, after working all day in the field, to come home and get the meals, and then, after that, have the family sewing to do. In our view, woman never was made to do the work which supports the family ; and, if she do it, the family suffers more for want of the mother's vitality expended in work than it gains in the wages she receives. Some of the brightest and most intelligent negro men begin to see this, and to remove their wives from field-labor ; but on the plantation, as we saw it, the absence of the mother all day from home was the destruction of any home-life or improvement.

Yet, with all this, the poor things, many of them, showed a most affecting eagerness to be taught to read and write. We carried down and distributed a stock of spelling-books among them, which they eagerly accepted, and treasured with a sort of superstitious veneration ; and

Sundays, and evenings after work, certain of them would appear with them in hand, and earnestly beg to be taught. Alas! we never felt so truly what the loss and wrong is of being deprived of early education as when we saw how hard, how almost hopeless, is the task of acquisition in mature life. When we saw the sweat start upon these black faces, as our pupils puzzled and blundered over the strange cabalistic forms of the letters, we felt a discouraged pity. What a dreadful piece of work the reading of the English language is! Which of us would not be discouraged beginning the alphabet at forty?

After we left, the same scholars were wont to surround one of the remaining ladies. Sometimes the evening would be so hot and oppressive, she would beg to be excused. "O misse, but two of us will fan you all the time!" And "misse" could not but yield to the plea.

One of the most dreaded characters on the place was the dairy-woman and cook Minnah. She had been a field-hand in North Carolina, and worked at cutting down trees, grubbing land, and mauling rails. She was a tall, lank, powerfully-built woman, with a pair of arms like windmill-sails, and a tongue that never hesitated to speak her mind to high or low. Democracy never assumes a more rampant form than in some of these old negresses, who would say their screed to the king on his throne, if they died for it the next minute. Accordingly, Minnah's back was all marked and scored with the tyrant's answers to free speech. Her old master was accustomed to reply to her unpleasant observations by stretching her over a log, staking down her hands and feet, and flaying her alive, as a most convincing style of argument. For all that, Minnah was neither broken nor humbled: she still asserted her rights as a human being to talk to any other human being as seemed to her good and proper ; and many an amusing specimen of this she gave us. Minnah had learned to do up gentlemen's shirts passably, to iron and to cook after a certain fashion, to make butter, and do some other household tasks : and so, before the wives of the gentlemen arrived on the place, she had been selected as a sort of general housekeeper and manager in doors ; and, as we arrived on the ground first, we found Minnah in full command, — the only female presence in the house.

It was at the close of a day in May, corresponding to our August, that Mrs. F—— and baby and myself, with sundry bales of furniture and household stuff, arrived at the place. We dropped down in a lazy little sail-boat which had lain half the day becalmed, with the blue, hazy shores on either side melting into indefinite distance, and cast anchor far out in the stream ;

and had to be rowed in a smaller boat to the long wharf that stretched far out into the waters. Thence, in the thickening twilight, we ascended, passed through the belt of forest-trees that over-hung the shore, and crossed the wide fields of fine white sand devoted to the raising of cotton. The planter's house was a one-story cottage, far in the distance, rising up under the shelter of a lofty tuft of Spanish oaks.

Never shall we forget the impression of weird and almost ludicrous dreariness which took possession of us as Mrs. F—— and my-self sat down in the wide veranda of the one-story cottage to wait for the gentlemen, who had gone down to assist in landing our trunks and furniture. The black laborers were coming up from the field ; and, as one and another passed by, they seemed blacker, stranger, and more dismal, than any thing we had ever seen.

The women wore men's hats and boots, and

had the gait and stride of men ; but now and then an old hooped petticoat, or some cast-off, thin, bedraggled garment that had once been fine, told the tale of sex, and had a wofully funny effect.

As we sat waiting, Minnah loomed up upon us in the twilight veranda like a gaunt Libyan sibyl, walking round and round, surveying us with apparent curiosity, and responding to all our inquiries as to who and what she was by a peculiarly uncanny chuckle. It appeared to amuse her extremely that Mr. F—— had gone off and left the pantry locked up, so that she could not get·us any supper ; we being faint and almost famished with our day's sail. The sight of a white baby dressed in delicate white robes, with lace and embroidery, also appeared greatly to excite her ; and she stalked round and round with a curious simmer of giggle, appearing and disappearing at uncertain intervals, like a black sprite, during the mortal hour and a half that it cost our friends to land the goods from the vessel.

After a while, some supper was got for us in a wide, desolate apartment, fitted up with a small cooking-stove in the corner.

Never shall we forget the experience of endeavoring to improvise a corn-cake the next morning for breakfast.

We went into the room, and found the table standing just as we had left it the night before, — not a dish washed, not a thing done in the way of clearing. On inquiry for Minnah, she was gone out to milking. It appeared that there were sixteen cows to be milked before her return. A little colored girl stood ready to wait on us with ample good nature.

" Lizzie," said we, " have you corn-meal ? "

" Oh, yes'm ! " and she brought it just as the corn had been ground, with the bran unsifted.

" A sieve, Lizzie."

It was brought.

" A clean pan, Lizzie. Quick ! "

" All right," said Lizzie : " let me get a pail of water." The water was to be drawn from a deep well in the yard. That done, Lizzie took a pan, went out the door, produced a small bit of rag, and rinsed the pan, dashing the contents upon the sand.

" Lizzie, haven't you any dish-cloth ? "

" No'm."

" No towels ? "

" No'm."

" Do you always wash dishes this way ? "

" Yes'm."

" Well, then, wash this spoon and these two bake-pans."

Lizzie, good-natured and zealous as the day is long, bent over her pail, and slopped and scrubbed with her bit of rag.

"Now for a pan of sour milk," said we.

It was brought, with saleratus and other condiments; and the cake was made.

But, on examination, the flues of the little cooking-stove were so choked with the resinous soot of the "light-wood" which had been used in it, that it would scarcely draw at all; and the baking did not progress as in our nice Stuart stove in our Northern home. Still the whole experience was so weirdly original, that, considering this was only a picnic excursion, we rather enjoyed it.

When we came to unpack china and crockery and carpets, bureau and bedsteads and dressing-glass, Minnah's excitement knew no bounds. Evidently she considered these articles (cast-off remnants of our Northern home) as the height of splendor.

When our upper chamber was matted, and furnished with white curtains and shades, and bed, chairs, and dressing-glass, Minnah came in to look; and her delight was boundless.

"Dear me! O Lord, O Lord!" she exclaimed, turning round and round. "Dese yer Northern ladies — they 'hes every thing, and they does every thing!"

More especially was she taken with the pictures we hung on the walls. Before one of these (Raphael's Madonna of the Veil) Minnah knelt down in a kind of ecstatic trance, and thus delivered herself:—

"O good Lord! if there ain't de Good Man when he was a baby! How harmless he lies there! so innocent! And here we be, we wicked sinners, turning our backs on him, and going to the Old Boy. O Lord, O Lord! we ought to be better than we be : we sartin ought."

This invocation came forth with streaming tears in the most natural way in the world; and Minnah seemed, for the time being, perfectly

20

subdued. It is only one of many instances we have seen of the overpowering influence of works of art on the impressible nervous system of the negro.

But it is one thing to have an amusing and picturesque specimen of a human being, as Minnah certainly was, and another to make one useful in the traces of domestic life.

As the first white ladies upon the ground, Mrs. F—— and myself had the task of organizing this barbaric household, and of bringing it into the forms of civilized life. We commenced with the washing.

Before the time of our coming, it had been customary for the gentlemen to give their washing into the hands of Minnah or Judy, to be done at such times and in such form and manner as best suited them.

The manner which *did* suit them best was to put all the articles to soak indefinitely, in soapsuds, till such time as to them seemed good. On being pressed for some particular article, and roundly scolded by any of the proprietors, they would get up a shirt, a pair of drawers, a collar or two, with abundant promises for the rest when they had time.

The helpless male individuals of the establishments had no refuge from the feminine ruses and expedients, and the fifty incontrovertible reasons which were always on hand to prove to them that things could be done no other way than just as they were done; and, in fact, found it easier to get their washing back again by blandishments than by bullying.

We ladies announced a regular washing-day, and endeavored to explain it to our kitchen cabinet; our staff consisting of Minnah and Judy, detailed for house-service.

Judy was a fat, lazy, crafty, roly-poly negress, the Florida wife of the foreman Mose, and

devoted to his will and pleasure in hopes to sup-
plant the "Virginny" and "Carliny" wives.
Judy said yes to every thing we proposed ; but
Minnah was "kinky" and argumentative : but
finally, when we represented to her that the
proposed arrangement was customary in good
Northern society, she gave her assent.

We first proceeded to make a barrel of soda
washing-soap in a great iron sugar-kettle, which
stood out under the fig-trees, and which had
formerly been used for evaporating sugar.

Minnah took the greatest interest in the
operation, and, when the soap was finished,
took the boiling liquid in pailfuls, setting them
on the top of her head, and marching off to the
barrel in the house with them, without ever
lifting a finger.

We screamed after her in horror, —

"Minnah, Minnah ! If that should fall, it
would kill you !"

A laugh of barbaric exultation was the only response, as she actually persisted in carrying pailful after pailful of scalding soap on her head till all was disposed of.

The next day the washing was all brought out under the trees and sorted, Mrs. F—— and myself presiding ; and soon Minnah and Judy were briskly engaged at their respective tubs. For half an hour, "all went merry as a marriage-bell." Judy was about half through her first tubful, when Mose came back from his morning turn in the fields, and summoned her to come home and get his breakfast. With Judy's very leisurely and promiscuous habits of doing business, this took her away for half the forenoon. Meanwhile, Minnah murmured excessively at being left alone, and more especially at the continuous nature of the task.

Such a heap of clothes to be washed *all in one day!* It was a mountain of labor in Minnah's imagination ; and it took all our eloquence and our constant presence to keep her in good humor. We kept at Minnah as the only means of keeping her at her work.

But, after all, it was no bad picnic to spend a day in the open air in the golden spring-time of Florida. The birds were singing from every covert ; the air was perfectly intoxicating in its dreamy softness ; and so we spread â camp for the baby, who was surrounded by a retinue of little giggling, adoring negroes, and gave ourselves up to the amusement of the scene. Our encampment was under the broad leaves of a group of fig-trees ; and we hung our clothes to dry on the sharp thorns of a gigantic clump of Yucca gloriosa, which made an admirable clothes-frame.

By night, with chuckling admiration, Minnah surveyed a great basketful of clean clothes, — all done in one day.

The next day came the lesson on ironing; and the only means of securing Minnah and Judy to constant work at the ironing-table was the exercise of our own individual powers of entertainment and conversation. We had our own table, and ironed with them; and all went well till Judy remembered she had preparations for Mose's dinner, and deserted. Minnah kept up some time longer; till finally, when we went in the next room on an errand, she improved the opportunity to desert. On returning, we saw Minnah's place vacant, a half-finished shirt lying drying on the table.

Searching and calling, we at last discovered her far in the distance, smoking her pipe, and lolling tranquilly over the fence of a small enclosure where were sixteen calves shut up together, so that maternal longings might bring the cow mothers home to them at night.

"Why, Minnah, what are you doing?" we said as we came up breathless.

"Laws, missis, I wanted to feed my calves. I jest happened to think on't." And forthwith she turned, started to the barn, and came back with a perfect hay-mow on her head. Then, crossing the fence into the enclosure, she proceeded to make division of the same among the calves, who tumultuously surrounded her. She patted one, and cuffed another, and labored in a most maternal style to make them share their commons equally; laughing in full content of heart, and appearing to have forgotten her ironing-table and all about it.

It was in vain to talk. "She was tired ironing. Did anybody ever hear of doing up all one's things in a day? Besides, she wanted to see her calves: she felt just like it." And Minnah planted her elbows on the fence, and gazed and smoked and laughed, and talked baby-talk to her calves, till we were quite provoked; yet we could not help laughing. In fact, long before that day was done, we were out of breath, used up and exhausted with the strain of getting the work out of Minnah. It was the more tantalizing, as she *could* do with a fair amount of skill any thing she pleased, and could easily have done the whole in a day had she chosen.

It is true, she was droll enough, in a literary and artistic view, to make one's fortune in a magazine or story; but, when one had a house to manage, a practical humorist is less in point than in some other places.

The fact was, Minnah, like all other women bred to the fields, abominated housework like a man. She could do here and there, and by fits and starts and snatches ; but to go on in any thing like a regular domestic routine was simply disgusting in her eyes. So, after a short period of struggle, it was agreed that Minnah was to go back to field-work, where she was one of the most valuable hands; and a trained house-servant was hired from Jacksonville.

Minnah returned to the field with enthusiasm. We heard her swinging her long arms, and shouting to her gang, "Come on, den, boys and gals! I'm for the fields! I was born, I was raised, I was fairly begot, in de fields; and I don't want none o' your housework."

In time we obtained a cook from Jacksonville, trained, accomplished, neat, who made beautiful bread, biscuit, and rolls, and was a comfort to our souls.

But this phœnix was soon called for by the wants of the time, and was worth more than we could give, and went from us to enjoy forty dollars per month as cook in a hotel.

Such has been the good fortune of all the well-trained house-servants since emancipation. They command their own price.

The untrained plantation hands and their

children are and will be just what *education* may make them.

The education which comes to them from the State from being freemen and voters, able to make contracts, choose locations, and pursue their own course like other men, is a great deal ; and it is operating constantly and efficaciously.

We give the judgment of a practical farmer accustomed to hire laborers at the North and the South ; and, as a result of five years' experiment on this subject, he says that the negro laborer *carefully looked after* is as good as any that can be hired at the North.

In some respects they are better. As a class they are more obedient, better natured, more joyous, and easily satisfied.

The question as to whether, on the whole, the negroes are valuable members of society, and increasing the material wealth of the State, is best answered by the returns of the Freedman's

Savings and Trust Company, — an institution under the patronage of government.

The report of this institution for the year 1872 is before us ; and from this it appears that negro laborers in the different Southern States have deposited with this Trust Company this year the sum of THIRTY-ONE MILLION TWO HUNDRED AND SIXTY THOUSAND FOUR HUNDRED AND NINETY-NINE DOLLARS.

The report also shows, that, year by year, the amount deposited has increased. Thus, in 1867, it was only $1,624,883 ; in 1868 it was three million odd ; in 1869 it was seven million and odd ; in 1870, twelve million and odd ; in 1871, nineteen million and odd.

These results are conclusive to the fact, that, as a body, the Southern laborers are a thrifty, industrious, advancing set ; and such as they are proved by the large evidence of these figures, such we have observed them in our more limited experience.

Our negro laborers, with all the inevitable defects of imperfect training, ignorance, and the negligent habits induced by slavery, have still been, as a whole, satisfactory laborers. They keep their contracts, do their work, and save their earnings. We could point to more than one black family about us steadily growing up to competence by industry and saving.

All that is wanted to supply the South with a set of the most desirable skilled laborers is simply education. The negro children are bright ; they can be taught any thing : and if the whites, who cannot bear tropical suns and fierce extremes, neglect to educate a docile race who both can and will bear it for them, they throw away their best chance of success in a most foolish manner. No community that properly and carefully educates the negro children now growing up need complain of having an idle, thriftless, dishonest population about them.

Common schools ought to prevent that. The teaching in the common schools ought to be largely industrial, and do what it can to prepare the children to get a living by doing something well. Practical sewing, cutting and fitting, for girls, and the general principles of agriculture for boys, might be taught with advantage.

The negroes are largely accused of being thievish and dishonest.

A priori we should expect that they would be so. We should imagine, that to labor without wages for generations, in a state of childish dependence, would so confuse every idea of right and wrong, that the negro would be a hopeless thief.

Our own experience, however, is due in justice to those we have known.

On the first plantation, as we have said, were about thirty families from all the different Southern States. It might be supposed that they were a fair sample.

Now as to facts. It was the habit of the family to go to bed nights, and leave the house doors unlocked, and often standing wide open. The keys that locked the provisions hung up in a very accessible place; and yet no robbery was ever committed. We used to set the breakfast-table over night, and leave it with all the silver upon it, yet lost nothing.

In our own apartment we put our rings and pins on our toilet-cushions, as had been our habit. We had bits of bright calico and ribbons, and other attractive articles, lying about; and the girl that did the chamber-work was usually followed by a tribe of little curious, observing negroes: and yet we never missed so much as a shred of calico. Neither was this because they did not want them; for the gift of a strip of calico or ribbon would throw them into raptures: it was simply that they did not steal.

Again : nothing is more common, when we visit at the North, than to have the complaint made that fruit is stolen out of gardens. We have had people tell us that the vexation of having fruit carried off was so great, that it took away all the pleasure of a garden.

Now, no fruit is more beautiful, more tempting, than the orange. We live in an orange-grove surrounded by negroes, and yet never have any trouble of this kind. We have often seen bags of fine oranges lying all night under the trees ; and yet never have we met with any perceptible loss. Certainly it is due to the negroes that we have known to say that they are above the average of many in the lower classes at the North for honesty.

We have spoken now for the average negro : what we have said is by no means the best that can with truth be said of the finer specimens among them.

We know some whose dignity of character, delicacy, good principle, and generosity, are admirable, and more to be admired because these fine traits have come up under the most adverse circumstances.

In leaving this subject, we have only to repeat our conviction, that the prosperity of the more Southern States must depend, in a large degree, on the right treatment and education of the negro population.

21

INDEX.

1